DEVELOPING LOCAL ECONOMIC STRATEGIES

CONTEMPORARY ISSUES IN SOCIAL SCIENCES

This is series addresses current debates in the Social Sciences.
Short books will be authored by experienced academics with active
research interests in the relevant areas. Collections of papers
reporting up-to-date research on a single issue or theme will also
form part of the series, as well literature reviews and evaluations of
public policy.

Current Titles

Pamela Abbott & Roger Sapsford :   Community Care for Mentally

Handicapped Children

Allan Cochrane :   Developing Local Economic Strategies

Doreen Massey :   Nicaragua

DEVELOPING LOCAL ECONOMIC STRATEGIES

edited by
ALLAN COCHRANE

Open University Press
Milton Keynes   -   Philadelphia

Open University Press

Open University Educational Enterprises Limited

12 Cofferidge Close

Stony Stratford

Milton Keynes MK11 1BY, England

and

242 Cherry Street

Philadelphia, PA 19106, USA

First published 1987

Copyright © Allan Cochrane 1987

British Library Cataloguing in Publication Data
Developing local economic strategies : some issues and ideas. -
(Contemporary issues in social sciences series).
1. Local government - Great Britain
2. Great Britain - Economic policy - 1945 -
I. Cochrane, Allan II. Series
352.1'2   JS3111

ISBN 0-335-15522-7

Library of Congress Cataloging-in-Publication Data
Developing local economic strategies: some issues and ideas
(Contemporary issues in social sciences series)
1. Great Britain - Economic policy - 1945
2. Local Government - Great Britain
3. Regional Planning - Great Britain.
    I. Cochrane, Allan. II. Series
HC256.6.D48   1987   87-22681
338.941 - DC19   CIP
ISBN 0-335-15227

Printed in Great Britain by J. W. Arrowsmith Ltd, Bristol.

CONTENTS

INTRODUCTION

In the 1980s, many of the most interesting and exciting innovations in economic and industrial policy have come not from the departments of central government, but from a small number of Labour controlled local authorities. This collection of papers focuses on just some of the issues raised by the new local authority initiatives, and, in particular, on the extent to which it is possible to achieve wider social objectives through the development of economic policies.

The papers were originally presented to a conference organized by a group of active researchers at the Open University (Conference on Local Economic Strategies, Parsifal College, December 17/18th, 1986). The conference brought together a range of officers, councillors and academics, and all of the papers benefited from the lively and extensive discussion which took place. We would like to thank all those who attended for the contributions they made, and hope that they find at least some of their arguments reflected in the papers which follow.

We at the Open University do not see ourselves as academics commenting from the outside, but as part of the policy debate. That is reflected in the papers which follow - particularly those of Doreen Massey and Maureen Mackintosh which start from direct experience in the Greater London Enterprise Board (GLEB) and the Greater London Council (GLC). As a group we hope to continue to make links with those developing local economic strategies on a day to day basis, since we believe that informed and regular interchange between us will benefit both the University and the local authorities.

The papers in this collection represent only a small part of the discussion at the conference and of our interests at the Open University. There is, for example, no discussion of local technology policies, nor of cooperative development; both areas in which we have a strong research base. The papers also concentrate heavily (although not exclusively) on the London experience which is intended to give a more focussed picture of one set of policies, but does not reflect any obsessively metropolitan concerns on our part. The development of local economic strategies in London has come to the end of one phase with the abolition of the GLC, and it is a good time to think about what has been achieved in the past and what new directions may be taken in the future.

The papers which follow consider the underlying theme of the collection in different policy areas and from different perspectives. The first paper, by Alan Clarke and Allan Cochrane, considers the overall experience of enterprise boards and the extent to which it has in practice been possible to escape from the financial orthodoxies of the market in the course of investment in the private sector. Doreen Massey assesses the successes and difficulties of one particular aspect of GLEB's investment policies, namely the extent to which it has been possible to impose equal opportunity conditions on investment. In the third paper, Maureen Mackintosh considers the potential for influencing patterns of public investment by looking at the (now historical) links between the GLC and London Transport. The previous two papers are concerned with ways of influencing the private sector through investment: Maureen Mackintosh raises questions about the extent to which private sector criteria currently influence public sector investment practice. Finally, Keith Jefferis and Mike Robinson, explicitly returning to issues raised more implicitly earlier, discuss ways in which criteria for investment might be altered to take account of social returns, as well as private profits.

We hope that this collection will be the first of many in this policy area. We are aware that we have only begun to scratch the surface in terms of the issues raised by local economic strategies. But we believe the issues are important and need to be developed, even if the national environment for local initiative may remain hostile for some time to come.

Allan Cochrane
JULY, 1987

1 INVESTING IN THE PRIVATE SECTOR: THE ENTERPRISE BOARD EXPERIENCE
Alan Clarke & Allan Cochrane

From economic development to economic intervention
The move by local authorities towards investment in the
private sector is a relatively recent one, despite isolated
examples from the mid-1970s, such as Nottinghamshire's
investment in the holiday firm, Horizon Midland, which were
responses to immediate crises. They were not part of any
overall strategy for intervention. Local authority
involvement in economic development was mainly based on the
provision of premises and serviced land, the attraction of
firms from other areas, and support for small firms. The
underlying assumption of the traditional approach was that
the council's task was to provide incentives and
infrastructural support for the firms it was trying to
attract, and to provide a pleasant environment for their
managers to live in.

During the 1970s there was a dramatic growth in this form of economic development activity at local level. By the end of the decade it would have been difficult to find any council which did not have an officer responsible for it and many had set up specialist committees or sub-committees, and specialist units within departments. A new profession of industrial development officers (IDOs) grew up on this basis. The IDOs sold themselves to local authorities – even on the left – as people who understood the private sector and could, therefore, sell the advantages of the authority to developers, industrialists and commercial estate agents. They also prided themselves on representing their target groups within the councils for which they worked – in a sense, interpreting the needs and demands of the private sector to an uncomprehending public sector. The IDOs closely identified themselves with their 'client group' of developers and industrialists, both because it made them part of a wider professional community within the development world and because they relied on a response from these 'clients' as a measure of success.

The consequence of this, of course, was that economic intervention was effectively undertaken on the terms determined by those 'clients'. Local authorities became glorified estate agents and bent over backwards to avoid putting too many obstacles (for example, in the form of planning restrictions) in the way of possible developers or mobile industry. After the mid-1970s, this was encouraged by circulars from central governments of both major parties which blamed industrial decline in the inner cities on the imposition of harsh planning controls.

Although economic development work was often characterised by a high degree of frenetic promotional activity, in fact it implied an almost entirely reactive and opportunist role for the local authority as it sought to identify what the market wanted and then did its best to provide it. There was no scope for authorities to develop economic policies or economic strategies. In a few cases authorities even set up independent - but council funded - economic development companies which acknowledged the separation between industrial development and the usual operations of local government. Councils did not try to put pressure on enterprises - except very small or environmentally unpleasant ones - to achieve change. Nor did they consider the impact of their own spending or employment on the local economy because the 'economy' was essentially defined as whatever was outside their direct influence.

There were few exceptions to these lines of approach, although Wandsworth did try to move in a rather different direction in the late 1970s, and ideas developed there fed into the policies later introduced at the Greater London Council (GLC). South Yorkshire also set up a County Regional Investment Scheme for the local investment of money from its employees' pension fund, which could be seen as a precursor of local enterprise boards, but the negligible extent of its investment makes it difficult to take it seriously as an economic initiative.

In its traditional form, economic development activity was largely undertaken outside political control and with little interest from politicians. Money would be allocated virtually on demand, because everybody agreed that it was important to try to do something about unemployment, but with very little detailed scrutiny over or interest in how the money was spent. The evidence of new industrial estates filled with tenants or of promotional activity in the form of glossy brochures was enough to assure councillors that something was being done. Economic development might be a 'good' thing supported by all but it did not have the political importance of social services, education or housing. It was not generally contentious between the parties.

It took the shock of Labour's massive defeat in 1979, the development of mass unemployment and the failure of Labour's industrial policy at national level during the 1970s to make some councils consider new ways of intervention at local level. At national level the new Conservative Goverment had rejected the idea of an industrial strategy, yet it became clear that the market would not generate new jobs on its own (even with the help of factory units built by the council). There was little 'footloose' industry to be attracted, however good an IDO's publicity campaign might be. Commitments to developing new approaches to economic development began to appear in local Labour manifestoes in the early 1980s, finding their first full expression in several of the councils newly elected in 1981. Five of the manifestoes of successful Labour groups included promises to set up local enterprise boards - in Greater London, Lancashire, Merseyside, the West Midlands and West Yorkshire. Each of these boards was to be set up as an independent body - a limited company - still linked to its parent authority but with specialist responsibilities for investment in the private sector and with no need to pass through the usual committee cycle before deciding on particular investments.

This commitment to a high degree of autonomy was not a reflection of a lack of political interest but, on the contrary, a reflection of the fear that without it new - political - initiatives would get lost in a morass of local bureaucracy. It assumed the appointment of specialist officers with a commitment to the new policies and no historical responsibility for those of the past. The new boards were not to be like the older economic development companies, responding to demands from developers and attempting to attract investment from the outside.

The new policies were developed from the political side of local government, rather than the officer side, which had previously dominated policy-making in this field. Indeed, the introduction of these policies could be seen as a major indictment of the ways in which the officers had operated in the past. It implied a more active local authority role, one in which the council would be able to influence the operation of firms through equity shareholding or the offer of loans, and one in which it made sense, for the first time, to talk of local authority *strategies*. Because of its particular origins the move towards investment in the private sector was generally seen to be a move to the left, although we shall argue that in practice state investment in the private sector has been undertaken from a wide range of political perspectives.

New policies and new ideas

The initial arguments for local enterprise boards, put most strongly by politicians associated with the Greater London Enterprise Board (GLEB) and the West Midlands Enterprise Board (WMEB), clearly came from the left, and from a left disillusioned by the experience of Labour in government between 1974 and 1979. There was explicit reference back to key elements of Labour's 1973 programme, with its support for a National Enterprise Board (NEB), but attempts were also made to learn from the NEB experience, which was interpreted rather negatively. The new boards were to start from a different basis.

There was to be a genuine commitment to restructuring industry, and above all, to intervention on the side of labour rather than capital. It was felt both that the NEB had not been prepared to intervene positively in the process of industrial restructuring (it had depended too much on crisis intervention without any overall strategy), and that when it had intervened it had done so on management terms. Indeed, the lack of any overall strategy was felt to have left the Board at the mercy of the major corporations in which it invested. The local authority based initiatives were to build on the experience of workers in industry and to be related to more coherent sectoral analyses. Economic restructuring, it was argued, was already taking place, at the expense of the unemployed according to the 'logic', of the market. This left ordinary people powerless in the face of apparently inexorable forces and state intervention was needed to counter these.

Secondly, there was to be a shift towards decentralized, locally based responses. Not (just) because, in the absence of a Labour government, there was no hope for any national initiative, but (also) because a positive alternative to centralized bureaucratic initiatives was needed. An important element of the left critique of the post-war experience of Labour in power was an attack on bureaucratic centralism, symbolized by the undemocratic (and inefficient) nationalized state monopolies. The left remained committed to state intervention as an alternative to the market, but wanted to develop it in such a way that it empowered ordinary people, instead of leaving them powerless. Planning agreements and enterprise planning were to involve workers and communities in identifying social needs and democratizing work processes.

A third crucial element of the early arguments for local enterprise boards arose out of the Wilson Committee on the operation of financial institutions. At present, it was argued, potentially profitable investments are being missed because of the short-sightedness and metropolitan focus of traditional investment institutions. Institutions in the City of London are more interested in short-term returns than in long-term investment. They have no particular loyalty to investment in itain, or to investment which will help to build a stro r British economy. In particular they are unlikely to invest significantly outside the South-East, East Anglia and the M4 corridor, or within the inner cities; and they have lit le interest in investment in small and medium-sized firms or in manufacturing industry. They are under no democratic control, yet they effectively determine the investment strategies of most workers' pension funds. It is argued that the state needs to intervene to encourage longer term investment which will help to regenerate British industry. There is a 'funding gap' - between what the private financial sector is prepared to invest in British industry and what could prifitably and productively be invested - which needs to be filled.

The key continuity with the NEB was a basic commitment to working through equity and other investment in the private sector to provide leverage for the achievement of particular economic and social policies. Later - in echoes of older slogans directed towards the state - this was described as working 'in and against the market'. The idea was that it was possible to use market mechanisms and market rules to undermine some of the worst aspects of market based decision-making in practice, and to show what alternatives might be developed. The informed intervention of the state on the side of the workers (or the community) at the level of the firm or sector rather than the level of the economy (on the Keynesian model) or on the basis of nationalization (on a bureaucratic socialist model) might allow a more fine grained but ultimately more effective process of change, which challenged the market, not by ignoring it (Keynes) nor by trying to substitute for it (old style nationalization) but by playing it at its own game. Processes of production, it was argued, could only be changed by intervening directly at the level of production, in a sort of socialist microeconomics.

Some important elements of the NEB model, of course, could not be borrowed by the local boards. That was not always explicitly recognized by local politicians in the late 1970s and early 1980s, when the discovery of powers to spend the product of a 2p rate under Section 137 of the Local Government Act seemed to offer remarkable riches, particularly to the GLC and the metropolitan councils looking for new policy areas to work in. The unfortunate necessity of developing local policies because there was little prospect of a Labour Government at national level was often hidden in rhetoric about democratization and the idea that 'local' intervention was somehow good in itself. Some have argued that any traditional 'top-down' approach on a national level, identifying priorities from above, will limit the possibility for 'bottom-up' initiatives which start from the experience of those working in industry. But whatever the rationale, the fact is that the 'top-down' approach was not even on offer to be rejected at local level.

Yet the initial arguments for the NEB (as expressed in Holland's 'The Socialist Challenge', for example) were based on the notion that the state could identify key firms in what Holland called the *meso* economic - or monopoly - sector, invest in them and positively influence their investment and employment strategies, ensuring that they acted as flagships for the new policies, forcing their competitors to follow them. It was this which gave the initial arguments for a National Enterprise Board their clearest socialist aspect. Such an approach was not possible, even for the most left wing of Labour councils, although without some influence at the *meso,* as well as the micro, level they would be competing unequally for attention with the major corporations on which many of the small and middle sized firms in the micro sector depended for orders and supplies.

The new boards

Both GLEB and WMEB were presented in clear political terms in the manifestoes which gave rise to them. They developed out of debates within the local parties, but each was also initially associated with strong political figures within the councils which set them up. In neither case was the board intended simply to be viewed as a local authority initiative. In their different ways, each was intended to provide a radical alternative to the old NEB which could and should be taken up by a new Labour government.

Even so, they started out from different political bases and their early experience further separated them, although external pressures in the wake of abolition may now be bringing them closer together. The early arguments for WMEB focused largely on problems of restructuring at a regional level. The key arguments were that the process of restructuring being encouraged by the market tended to disadvantage the West Midlands, and, in particular, tended to benefit foreign competitors of the region's main producers. The logic of the market was to withdraw funds and seek short-term returns elsewhere, instead of investing to encourage long-term growth, for example by supporting effective rationalization within industrial sectors, including mergers and support for the most efficient firms. In other words in the West Midlands the market was not taking up the task of restructuring which it might normally be expected to do. Even the policies of the NEB within the region seemed to have reinforced this, by slicing up British Leyland (BL) into more and more parts until bits of it could be sold off and the industry as a whole left decimated. WMEB's policies were to be the reverse: identifying long-term growth prospects and building on success within the region. It would be able to take an industry-wide and region-wide approach. At the centre of WMEB's philosophy was the view that Labour's national approach to the regeneration of British industry through selective investment could work, if only it were targetted accurately enough and given sufficient support.

The critique of Labour's past which lay behind GLEB's formation was rather more extensive, and was developed further within the GLC's Economic Policy Group which was closely involved with GLEB. Certainly, GLEB shared WMEB's concern with restructuring, and has attempted to identify key areas of investment to encourage change within particular industrial sectors, such as furniture. But, at the heart of its wider critique was the view that it was necessary not only to encourage the reorganization of industry around potential growth poles, but also to challenge internal organization and decision-making structures within enterprises. The guidelines passed on by the GLC to GLEB included a set of criteria for investment which ranged from commercial viability to equal opportunity policies, the development of 'socially useful products' and new forms of 'social ownership'. A complex system of enterprise planning was envisaged for GLEB's investments, in which there was expected to be regular liaison between GLEB, representatives of the workforce and management. The process of enterprise planning was intended to encourage the involvement of workers in decision-making and to make long-term monitoring an active relationship, rather than one merely reflected in balance sheets or reports from management.

Whatever the differences between them, however, both GLEB and WMEB started with the desire to act as demonstration projects to be taken up more widely by a Labour government in the future - now apparently an increasingly distant future. And this was reflected in their ambitions, and their explicit references to restructuring industries and regions.

The other first wave enterprise boards - Lancashire Enterprises Limited (LEL), Merseyside Enterprise Board (MEB) and West Yorkshire Enterprise Board (WYEB) - although also launched by Labour authorities, have always been less concerned to present themselves as new political models. Ironically perhaps that probably makes them more attractive as models for a future Labour government, since it makes them look more like the National Investment Bank, which appears in Labour's most recent programmes, than a radical National Enterprise Board seeking to alter the face of British capitalism, and move towards a socialist model. Their methods have also been widely taken up by other local authorities, including several not controlled by Labour. Kent County Council, for example, has absorbed them into its economic development company without any pretensions to radicalism. These methods are not necessarily incompatible with traditional or mainstream models of local authority intervention, just because of their historical origins on the left, so that the offer of equity funding becomes just another incentive capable of attracting new development.

Among the 'first wave' boards, LEL's approach builds most clearly on the traditional approach to local authority economic development work, but transforms it into a more coherent and integrated package. Unlike the other boards - with the partial exception of GLEB before the abolition of the GLC - LEL has responsibility for all the council's economic policy, and remains tied to the county council both because some of its activities are funded by it and because it has a formal responsibility to report back to the council's policy and resources committee. Even before the abolition of their parent authorities in 1986, the other boards had a higher degree of formal autonomy and were more specialist investment arms.

LEL's position is probably closest to what could be called mainstream Labour politics. It explicitly presents itself as taking a pragmatic view of local possibilities, eschewing any attempts to put new demands on those who borrow from it, but stressing its willingness to adopt more flexible attitudes to investment than are usual from traditional financial institutions. It sees itself as a catalyst, able to mobilize additional funds as a result of its ability to put together convincing packages to the private sector, or to the European Social Fund. Because its leading officers (and associated councillors) see themselves as untrammelled by unnecessary political prejudice, it is able to offer itself as a sensible and no-nonsense agency, linked to the unions, but also open to the arguments of bankers in their areas of expertise. It takes on the image of a severely practical institution, which is nonetheless prepared to consider - and even put together - unusual proposals, as it did, for example, in putting together support for a management buy-out of BL Trucks. Although its proposal for BL Trucks was ultimately unsuccessful, the very fact that it could put one together was an indication of the width of its financial base and its political confidence.

If LEL has most clearly retained its local authority base in terms of the range of its activities, WYEB has always emphasised one aspect of the enterprise board model at the expense of any others. It stresses that it is essentially a publicly funded, regionally based merchant bank, using the same sort of criteria for investment as other financial institutions and with little concern for social criteria in its decision-making on individual investments. The assumption is, of course, that the board's investments will create jobs and it is an assumption shared by the other boards. What is needed, it is argued, is a regionally based source of funds for investment to overcome current obstacles to investment, to fill the 'funding gap'. MEB which is the most recently set up and the most modestly funded of the boards - with, arguably, the biggest task - has generally taken a similar view, stressing the care with which it scrutinizes all applications for financial support.

The key argument here - and it is in principle one shared by GLEB and WMEB - is that a regional base is required if investment funds are to be prised out of the City of London for use in regions like West Yorkshire and Merseyside, in manufacturing industry, in the inner cities or in enterprises which do not fit the prejudices of the institutions - such as worker cooperatives and black businesses. At present, it is argued, potentially profitable investments are being missed by Britain's dominant financial institutions. This creates new opportunities for local enterprise boards, because it implies that they can make profits from their own investments, which can then be reinvested to ensure the financial survival of the boards themselves. This is more important now than ever because since the abolition of the GLC and the metropolitan county councils none of the boards - with the possible exception of LEL - can any longer expect to receive substantial financial support from a local authority.

But this argument was always at the heart to WYEB's approach. It was not expected to receive significant support from the West Yorkshire County Council, and its officers were always the most commercially oriented.

A second element in the argument that profitable investments are there and are being missed is that if the boards can indeed identify them, then they may be able to have a wider impact on the operation of investors. This has been argued most strongly by WYEB, but is an element in the work of all the boards. It is hoped that other (private sector) financial isntitutions can be shown the error of their ways in practice by the success of the boards. One of the central aims of all the boards is to identify ways of 'levering' additional funds out of the private sector, and most of them also attempt to attract finance for investment from pension funds. But a real sign of success would be if financiers began to invest in the same areas as the boards without their support although, of course, that would mean forgetting any social aims. The problem of competition for profitable investment is one which would in principle be welcomed by the boards, although it might make their day to day activities in identifying profitable investments a little more difficult. The hope is, of course, that successful investment will generate self-sustaining growth and the creation of more investment opportunities.

Problems and prospects

Investing in the private sector has been a risky business for all the boards. This risk is exacerbated by the parts of the private sector in which the boards invest. The enterprises tend to be relatively weak, which is why they approach the boards rather than more established financial institutions in the first place. The enterprises in which the boards invest are generally middle sized (ie employing over fifty people) rather than small or corporate. But many of these middle sized firms are characterized by a rather conservative management style, often family firms which have ceased to grow and have lost the dynamism of their founders. Ironically, that dynamism sometimes has to be reintroduced not by the private sector but through the intervention of an enterprise board. There is not some dynamic enterprise culture out there waiting to spring up when constraints are removed, as is suggested by the approach of the Thatcher Government. On the contrary the experience of the boards shows that it needs to be created by external pressure.

Business plans are now paramount for all the boards in the assessment of investment proposals. Two considerations are important in the consideration of these: first, the projections of commercial viability and secondly - and equally important - the managerial skills of those involved. The vital point about the preparation of business plans is not the balance sheets and projections they produce but the information they provide about the management abilities of those who have prepared them. The experience of all the boards confirms that as well as a 'funding gap' - indeed probably more significant than any 'funding gap' - there is what Doreen Massey has called a 'management gap', which the boards have often been forced to try to fill, by introducing management changes within enterprises. Sometimes officers of the boards have themselves taken over direct management responsibility.

Another factor increasing risk is that, not only are entrepreneurs notoriously optimistic about their prospects when seeking financial support, but some have proved to be deliberately dishonest, relying on enterprise board funds not for investment but as an immediate source of income. Unfortunately, the failure of a relatively small number of investments can have a disproportionately dramatic effect on the portfolio of any of the boards. In the circumstances, the returns achieved by the boards on their investments have been quite impressive.

The risks of investment have, however, forced some boards
away from their more ambitious aims and encouraged others in
their less ambitious ones. The most confident boards today
seem to be LEL and WYEB. They are being followed by private
sector institutions, either in partnership or - still more
flattering - in imitation. Regionally based investment funds
are now being set up by banks and other financial
institutions. They have even been successful in themselves
attracting funding from banks, to invest on their behalf.
Despite a change in political control within Lancashire
County Council, LEL has survived relatively unaffected
because of its successful links outside the council. And
WYEB has used the abolition of West Yorkshire County Council
as an opportunity to spread its net wider to the region as a
whole, and how has no formal links of accountability to any
local authority. It is prepared to survive on its income and
funds raised within the private sector, and has been approved
as an enterprise agency by the Department of Industry.

GLEB which was - arguably - the most politically
confident board and the one most often understood to be the
model for enterprise boards, at least on the left, is now
less confident and subject to the most internal questioning.
Even before the abolition of the GLC, it largely turned in on
itself; rescuing previous investments or being forced to let
them go under. It had insufficient funds to support some of
the firms in which it had invested, and was increasingly
drawn into detailed rescues of many of those which were left.
Several of GLEB's executives were effectively working as
managers of firms in which GLEB's money had been invested.
As part of a programme of long-term restructuring this might
have been a positive shift, but in practice it was more of a
response to immediate crises.

GLEB found it increasingly difficult to implement its
wider social policies. It was difficult for one agency on
its own to shift the investment priorities of the private
sector. Some of the difficulties of introducing an equal

opportunities policy through the board's investments are discussed in Doreen Massey's paper in this collection. Enterprise planning, too, was difficult to develop since a frequent prerequisite was the creation of organizations capable of representing the workforce's views. In many cases trade union organization was very weak. Frequently, too, the GLEB structure and its investment concerns tended to mean that the board moved in from the top - ie via management, which approached GLEB, who fitted them into a sectoral approach, or intervened to rescue the enterprise from collapse.

In practice, the social criteria were always difficult to apply, but, because they were institutionalized within the system, there were major internal debates on several investments. Only within GLEB was there any accepted role for such criteria, backed by powerful political support within the GLC, the board of directors (appointed by the GLC) and among senior staff. It is easy to exaggerate the significance of this, since even the strongest supporters of GLEB's moves towards 'social cost accounting' would acknowledge that progress was limited, but there can be little doubt that since the abolition of the GLC and the changes within GLEB which accompanied it, the board has become less interested in such concerns. A decision has now been made to separate social and commercial criteria in the assessment of investment proposals, in part to acknowledge that otherwise commercial criteria come to dominate. The idea is that the costs of any socially oriented policies will be met separately, rather than being included in conditions attached to investments. Although in principle this move could be viewed as a positive reaffirmation of the importance of social criteria for investment, confirming that their costs need to be taken into account and not just wished away, in practice it looks more like a confirmation that they are expected to take second place to commercial criteria. More important, the change implies that local authorities are not in a strong bargaining position within the market. They cannot expect to be able to impose conditions significantly different from those imposed by other financial institutions.

Although the changes are less clear, the main emphasis of WMEB's work has also changed. After some early investments intended to encourage the restructuring of parts of the foundry industry in the West Midlands, at least one of which became a major drain on the board's resources, WMEB, like LEL and WYEB, has increasingly turned towards developing contacts with and proving itself to the existing financial institutions. Like the other two, it has become quite successful in that role. WMEB no longer makes any claims to restructuring, but instead stresses its role as a 'democratically controlled' regional development agency. It continues to specialise in manufacturing investment, but otherwise emphases its good relations with banks and other investment institutions. Since abolition, however, WMEB has also sustained a higher political profile than boards like WYEB. Like LEL, it claims to represent its region in industrial matters, and has built a strong base from which to do so. Since the abolition of the West Midlands County Council, it has successfully absorbed the Council's research and policy staff.

All of the boards now point to their favourable leverage ratios - ie the amount of private sector money they can lever out per investment (on recent figures it ranges from 1:2 and 1:5 between the boards, although the ways in which it is estimated also varies between them so comparison is not really possible). This emphasis on leverage ratios symbolizes the direction which the enterprise boards have taken since their foundation. It clearly benefits those for whom this has always been a central aim, and encourages those for whom it has not to change the emphasis of their policies - to cooperate with the private sector rather than challenge its priorities. LEL and WYEB point to the funds they have attracted from the private sector for onward investment by the boards.

Investment in the private sector has not been able to give local agencies the clear interventionist role some hoped for. In all cases commercial criteria are of crucial importance, if boards are to be able to survive with limited new finance. Not quite 'in and against the market', more 'in the market, to make it work a bit better at no real cost to investors'. In policy terms, they differ from private sector institutions in a number of ways which are quite important for previously excluded groups - in particular, they are filling some sort of a 'funding gap' in certain geographical areas and industrial sectors, but the importance of this gap does not seem to have been as great as they originally believed. With the possible exception of GLEB in its moments of deepest financial crisis, it appears that their limited funds have nevertheless been adequate to achieve their tasks, since they all proudly point out that no suitable investments have been turned down for lack of funds, and that they only fund some 2-3 per cent of the proposals which are made to them. In addition, they have a sympathy for worker cooperatives, which it is argued also have a better survival rate than most small firms; a sympathy for applications from ethnic minorities and, sometimes, women's enterprises. None of this should be belittled, but nor should its significance as a left initiative be exaggerated.

The development of any more extensive intervention, would require the existence of a wider national framework, in which it is - or should be - possible to identify target sectors and major enterprises within them for development. On this basis it would be possible to develop enterprise planning and planning agreements which are not trapped at the level of firms more concerned with daily survival than any agreements with local enterprise boards. On the other hand, the local enterprise board experience has shown that planning agreements need not be trapped behind the doors of boardrooms or in the offices of Whitehall. They have shown that it is possible and necessary to draw on local experiences and integrate locally based boards, involving workers at plant level and communities at local authority level and below. They have also shown the need for systematic assessment of possibilities rather than wishful thinking. The identification of targets should not take place on the basis of some abstract assessment of the economy, but should arise from local and national debates within the official and 'unofficial' trade union movement, as well as community organizations, possibly channelled through local authorities. Planning agreements could be given a real life if operated on this scale.

2 EQUAL OPPORTUNITIES: THE GLEB EXPERIENCE
Doreen Massey

The purpose of this paper is to reflect upon the experience of the Greater London Enterprise Board in its attempts during its early years of existence to introduce policies of equal opportunities into its investments. Because the aim of the paper, and of the conference, is to learn from these experiences, the focus here will be on the problems. This is not to say that there were not successes; indeed there were many, both in the specific area of equal opportunities and in social objectives more generally. Much of what will be discussed in this paper is indeed relevant to social objectives as a whole, as well as more specifically to equal opportunities. The focus, as has been said, is on the issue of equal opportunities within GLEB's investment portfolio.

When GLEB was established it was given two, rather different, objectives. The first was to create and maintain jobs within the London economy, achieving commercial viability within a period of two years on any investment. This objective is now generally referred to as the 'commercial objective'. Secondly, the aim was to improve the quality of employment within London, this to include equal opportunities. This objective is the one which came to be known as the 'social objective'. In the early years there was much unclarity about the relationship between these two objectives. The questions of how they were to be prioritised against each other, and of whether or not they were mutually contradictory, were rarely explicitly discussed. In practice therefore the two objectives maintained an uneasy and changing relationship, and on reflection much of the experience of the early years can be seen as an attempt to work out in practice how in fact the two objectives related to each other.

This ambiguity about the relationship between the two objectives led to a number of difficulties. Firstly there was some tendency to counterpose the two objectives in terms of a dichotomy between the 'realism' (i.e. the constraints of the market economy) of the commercial objective and the 'idealism', academicism or intellectualism of the social objective. Being able to read company accounts was consistently seen as 'tough', while social objectives were occasionally referred to as 'soft' and, on one now famous occasion, 'wishy washy'. There was much talk of the need for skilled personnel in relation to the commercial objective, but much less recognition of the need for skilled personnel in relation to the social objective. To some extent this represented a real situation. The social objective is much less easily quantifiable, indeed much less easily set down in any formal terms at all, than is the commercial objective. It did therefore for a long time remain more vague. However, this does not mean that it is more easy to deal with, rather that it is more difficult. Both on the board of GLEB, and more widely within the organization, there was a lack of understanding of the intellectual and political challenge of the issues of social objectives. Secondly, another way in which the two objectives related, was that on occasions social criteria would be used simply to 'soften' the operation of the commercial objective. When this was done without there being any clear social targets, it was simply a retreat from one objective without any clear advance being made towards the other. Thirdly there was, and still tends to be, a tendency to see success and failure solely in commercial terms. It is hard, precisely because of the lack of quantifiable targets, to see social failure and success in quite the same decisive terms.

Apart from these issues which relate to the double nature of the objectives set for GLEB a range of other problems was also encountered in the operation of equal opportunities, and more widely social, objectives. There were organisational difficulties: for a long time equal opportunities policies were far too dependent for their implementation on the individual good will of particular people within the organisation. There was no adequate structure for their implementation and enforcement. There were huge difficulties of enforcement and monitoring, and of countering resistence from management in the enterprises where we were investing. There were clear cases where management was so eager to get the investment which GLEB could provide, that they were prepared to agree to anything, but without really reckoning on having to fulfil the conditions. Enforcement of equal opportunities policies was difficult enough in those situations where GLEB had control over the company in ownership terms; in cases where this was not true, enforcement was virtually impossible. The implementation of equal opportunities policies also faced conflicts of interest within the labour movement. This was particularly the case because equal opportunities policies were at first both

designed and implemented through the process of Enterprise
Planning. That is, the policies were to be the product of
joint negotiations between GLEB, the workers in the
enterprise and the management. This hit a number of
difficulties. First of all, enterprise planning itself
turned out to be a much longer, more difficult and tortuous
process than had initially been envisaged. For that reason
equal opportunities policies were slow to develop. Second,
however, this very structure meant that equal opportunities
policies were to be drawn up by people already working in the
enterprises where GLEB had investments. Since one of the
aims of GLEB investment might be to broaden the spectrum of
workers involved in the enterprise, this posed immediate
problems. It might involve, for instance, challenges to
existing ways of working and recruitment. It might involve
challenging apprenticeship systems, for example; or systems
of recruitment from union lists. There were certainly some
successes in dealing with these potentially very serious
conflicts of interest, but such issues held up the design
and implementation of equal opportunities policies in a good
number of investments.

A further issue of concern about equal opportunities
policies revolved around the Interim Appraisal Criteria,
which GLEB had from the beginning as a means of selection of
investments. These criteria included a set of premia. The
premia were 'awarded' to potential investments on the basis
of certain social characteristics; for instance the
proportion of ethnic minorities, or women, that they
employed. Scoring high on these sets of premia would imply
that the amount of investment per job which an enterprise
could claim would be raised. It soon became clear that there
were a number of problems with the operation of these premia.
In fact it seems that, at least in the early years, the
maximum level of investment per job was actually rarely
reached on the initial investment anyway. In other words,
the operation of the premia did not significantly shift

the spectrum of enterprises within GLEB's overall portfolio. Moreover, on examination, the portfolio turned out very much not to be dominated by firms employing a majority of white males. Further it soon came to be realised that while these premia might in principle be a workable method of aiding in the process of selection of investments, what was really needed was a way of selecting firms which related not so much to their existing characteristics as to the potential which they embodied for the implementation of equal opportunities strategies. There may, for instance, be more room for progress on equal opportunities in a firm initially dominated by white male skilled workers, than in one dominated by black and/or female workers.

All these issues provoked discussion, if somewhat intermittently, within GLEB. And much was learned. There came to be agreement that investments could be failed on social grounds, and agreement that equal opportunities (or at least reaching a minimum level of equal opportunities agreements) should be a separate requirement from that of enterprise planning. This would have two effects. First, equal opportunities would be removed from the long-drawn-out process of enterprise plannning, in which only existing workers are involved. Secondly, some level of adherence to equal opportunities would not be a subject for negotiation; it would be a requirement prior to investment. Again, in recognition of some of the early organisational difficulties, equal opportunities, though still grossly understaffed, is as a division now centrally placed within GLEB. Finally, projects are now to have individually-tailored social plans, with properly laid out and measurable targets and dates, together with services and advice available to aid in their achievement. This should greatly increase the possibility of both monitoring and enforcement.

Some more fundamental issues

In many ways, then, GLEB reflected upon and learned from some of its early difficulties in the design and implementation of equal opportunities objectives. It remained, however, up against some more fundamental and structural difficulties. Two of these will be discussed below.

The first of these really concerns GLEB's very formation as an institution. This has deeply affected the kind of portfolio which it has been able to build up. As the previous section indicated, there has been considerable progress on the design and implementation of equal opportunities policies at the level of the individual project. What has been more difficult, and far less clearly addressed, is the issue of how to incorporate equal opportunities policies in the design of the overall portfolio. Clearly, the selection of sectors, the operation of premia in the selection of firms (referred to above), and the operation of policies such as support for black-led businesses, are all part of this design. But a strategy for intervention in the local economy which actually _started_ from GLEB's commitment to equal opportunities might produce very different criteria for selecting a portfolio from the ones which have been in operation so far. The feminist literature, to take one example, provides considerable discussion of the kinds of things which can be done; and a number of these were incorporated in the London Industrial Strategy. Even conceptualising 'the local economy' can turn out very differently if one starts, not from the sectoral divisions and definitions of work handed down to us by capital, but from what the London Industrial Strategy calls 'an economics geared to need'. Another way of putting the same thing is to talk of the conceptualisation of the economy as the reproduction of community in the fullest sense. If that is done, then, as the London Industrial Strategy points out, domestic labour becomes the most important sector of the economy in terms of time expended. Out of 280 million hours work done reproducing London every year only 100 million hours is paid for. 180 million hours - that is almost two-thirds of the work - is unpaid labour, primarily domestic. 'Yet', says the London Industrial Strategy, 'in spite of its importance the household is regarded as somehow outside the economy by traditional economists and rarely, if ever, does it make its appearance as part of an economic strategy'. The London Industrial Strategy goes on to analyse how the economy of London's households is in crisis, and concludes the section by saying 'for an economics centred around finance these issues are marginal. For an economics centred around need they should be our starting point ' (LIS paragraphs 1.57-1.66).

In spite of this, GLEB, which was to be one of the main instruments for the implementation of the GLC's economic strategy, was established in such a way as to make it structurally unable to work around an economics geared to need. The stumbling block is the nature of its commercial objective: the commitment to commercial viability within the space of two years for each individual investment. Such an objective means that GLEB cannot challenge the conception of the economy, which is one of the most capitalist things about it; nor can it change the boundary between what is 'economic' and what is 'social'. The economic is defined in terms of that which will produce a commercial financial return. This division between economic and social was enshrined in the division between GLEB and the GLC. GLEB was to produce the economic investments, and the GLC would provide grant finance for social programmes. This meant that GLEB, as in so many other ways, was unable to change the shape of the economy. The socialisation of domestic labour, for instance, through the provision of laundries or creches, was not within its scope, precisely because they could not in the short-run be profitable sectors. It is precisely their current location outside of the 'economic' which means that the competition which they face is from unpaid, generally female, labour.

For this reason, provision of such facilities - i.e. the creation of a new sector of production - is extremely expensive and will therefore need subsidising if the facilities are not to remain available only to those with high incomes. Any economic strategy which aims to go beyond the formalities of equal opportunities, to produce an anti-sexist programme of intervention, will have to think about the very shape of the economy itself, and about the division between what is currently called economic and what is currently called social. As it stands at the present, GLEB is unable to pursue an equal opportunities policy of this type.

The second structural constraint which GLEB faces in the implementation of its equal opportunities strategies, and social objectives more generally, again revolves around the nature of its commercial objective. Here the concern is with the investment in an individual enterprise. Assume that a firm has been selected for investment, has fulfilled all the criteria, and an individually-tailored social plan has been drawn up for implementation. The question remains: how will the implementation of this social plan be paid for? Almost all aspects of serious equal opportunities policies have costs attached to them, whether they be costs in terms of time, or of money. In the early days, the issue of the financing of social plans was barely considered explicitly. This was in part because of the reigning ambiguity about the relationship between the two objectives, and in part because clearly specified social plans were anyway only rarely drawn up for individual enterprises. Implicitly, it is probably fair to say that the assumption was that the firm itself would pay. In fact, even where there were clear objectives to be achieved, there was frequently neither the time nor the money within the enterprise to get serious social programmes going. In part at first this was explained by the fact that most of the firms in which GLEB was investing were financially marginal. This indeed is likely to be true of a high proportion of firms which enterprise boards fund. But the problem is not confined to such firms; the competition of the market would mean that extra costs loaded onto an enterprise are anyway going to be a problem whatever the circumstances. More recently, debate within GLEB seems to be coming round to the idea of dividing the budget allocated to any individual enterprise into two distinct parts: the first to be a clear commercial investment demanding a rate of return, and the second a grant for defined social purposes.

This formulation, although certainly much clearer than the woolly operation of the past, in its turn also raises a number of issues. First of all, and in relation to the previous discussion, it means that GLEB is, far from challenging the current given distinction between economic and social, explicitly reinforcing it. Secondly, and more practically, it will not always be possible simply to separate social costs from investment monies demanding a rate of return. Thirdly, and probably positively, this separation between investment and grant highlights even more the difficulties with the most 'obvious' criteria of GLEB's success - of numbers of jobs and cost per job. Cost per job is a criterion of success which has anyway been subject to a good deal of criticism. It is clearly important to raise when discussing the cost of an investment which creates or maintains jobs in relation to what would have been the cost of unemployment. It is more difficult to use, however, in competition with other economic initiatives, for instance enterprise zones. GLEB's commitment to creating decent jobs must mean that its jobs will cost more. Separating the budget into investment and social elements might allow that point to be made more forcibly. Having separately-costed social plans, moreover, will also make clear that there is some choice between numbers of jobs and quality of jobs; a commitment to better jobs will also mean that the number of investments overall will be reduced.

Fourthly, however, and more importantly, the separation of the budget into economic and social has implications for the nature of GLEB's political project. GLEB initially formulated its political aim in terms of a commitment to 'exemplary projects'. GLEB's investments would show how firms might be. There was an assumption that the kind of thing that GLEB was doing could be spread more widely throughout the economy. This was a reflection, yet again, of an implicit assumption that the commercial and social objectives could be added on to each other; and further that both of them were compatible with continuing to exist in a sea of market forces. Separating commercial and grant money is in a sense explicitly saying that projects are not now exemplary in the same way. That is, the positive characteristics cannot be expected to spread more widely amongst other firms in the economy. But this in turn has further implications. It means that the grant-funded social plans within GLEB's portfolio amount to no more than a set of social additions within those individual firms. They do not amount to an equal opportunities <u>strategy</u> which is expected to have implications more widely. In other words they amount to a series of improvements within firms, without those firms necessarily having been selected as the best place to introduce them. <u>Had we started</u> with equal opportunities as a strategy for selecting firms we might well have picked a completely different set of firms to subsidise – we might for instance have opted for expanding firms where there were more opportunities to intervene, for instance, in training and recruitment.

The fifth implication of this decision to divide investment is closely related to the fourth. If social plans are to be subsidised through grants, then they will imply, not just the control and ownership which the difficulties of enforcement have already been mentioned as requiring, but also a long term involvement with each enterprise. Properly drawn-up social plans will anyway take a long time to put into operation. And if their operation is subsidised, then it is clear that GLEB cannot simply withdraw from investments when it has turned them round commercially; what it is involved in is building up a gradually expanding portfolio of firms with progressive equal opportunities strategies. The way in which such a portfolio could be 'exemplary' is by forming a basis for wider programmes of campaigning.

This paper started by referring to GLEB's twin objectives. Thoughout the discussion an important element has been the ambiguity in the relationship between these two objectives. A common view is that the two are in simple opposition. On the one hand there is a need for commercial viability; on the other hand social improvements cost money, and are thereby a drain on the possibilities of commercial viability. This opposition is sometimes counterposed quite starkly in relation to accumulation. In this formulation the commercial objective reflects public intervention with the aim of promoting accumulation in capitalist terms, while the social objective has as its aim that of changing the relations of production. This formulation is in turn based on an analysis which would argue that, in relation to their commercial objectives, the function of enterprise boards such as GLEB is to step in where the market, or other characteristics of local capitalism, are not functioning properly. In GLEB's case there have been two particular strands to this argument: that there exists a finance gap, and that there are large areas of the London economy in decline simply because of a lack of good management. In other words, the analysis is that capitalism is working badly, and that GLEB could do better. There is no doubt some element of truth in this argument, and no doubt either that the malfunctionings of British capitalism do indeed provide a toehold for intervention on the part of agencies such as GLEB. But it can only be a toehold. The problems of unemployment in so many local areas of the British economy do not arise because of a malfunctioning of capitalism; they arise precisely as part of its functioning. If that is the case, however, then the relationship between the commercial and social objectives of an institution such as GLEB cannot be as postulated above. Even the creation and maintenance of employment becomes a 'social' objective. If this is so, we are once again faced - as in so many of the discussions in this seminar - with the necessity to formulate different methods of accounting from those currently in use in the private sector and the enterprise boards. Moreover this is the case not only for equal opportunities, and social objectives more widely, but for the very process of rebuilding local economies.

3 PLANNING THE PUBLIC SECTOR: AN ARGUMENT FROM THE CASE OF TRANSPORT IN LONDON
Maureen Mackintosh

The argument

Consider the following argument. We have at the moment - and have had for a long time - an unplanned public sector of the economy. What I mean by this statement is the following. Since the war, public sector services and industries have been administered and managed, individually, with variable efficiency. Planning and management systems have been instituted within the various organizations. But this group of firms and services, which form still a very substantial part of the production activity in our economy, have generally not been planned, in the sense of developed and coordinated with a wider set of economic purposes in mind.

This statement immediately needs some qualification. The individual services and industries, and aspects common to all of them such as pay levels, have been used sporadically by all governments for wider economic ends: influencing real income distribution, for example, or control of inflation. During the Thatcher governments, privatization and contracting out have been used, not merely as a method of changing the operation of individual services or industries, but in the service of a more general attempt to change the operation of the economy, for example by influencing the operation of the labour market, including the powers of unions.

But up to 1979, and indeed up to now among many people involved in public sector management, there has been a general presumption that the individual public sector services and industries should not be used for ends beyond themselves. Activities such as those listed in the last paragraph are widely seen as the interference of politicians in what should be independent financial and managerial decisions. Such an argument has been one line of attack, from opponents of the present government's policies for the public sector.

There is some evidence - though it would require a much longer paper to document this fully - that the view that individual public sector activities should be managed as independently as possible of politicians and their wider economic policies, has developed a progressively stronger life since the war. It has been reinforced by the increasing professionalization of the management of the public services, in the sense of the creation of specialized 'professionals' who are trained in the analysis and management of particular services. It has been further encouraged by the development of a specific body of economic analysis - based on neo-classical competition and welfare theory - which appeared to provide criteria for pricing and investment decisions which took in certain aspects of the wider economic social impact of public sector spending and investment without requiring coordination between industries and services. And it was solidified by a process of public expenditure planning at national level which asked no hard questions about the interrelation of spending decisions in different areas, and which denied to local councils the right and capacity to coordinate a large part of the public spending in their areas.

This progressive fragmentation of economic decision making within the public sector has laid some of the basis for present government policies. It had already formed one of the causes of a process of public sector economic decline, especially in the effectiveness of public sector service provision. It had also produced an acceptance of fragmented management and decision making, of which privatization, and more market-based criteria of operation, appeared to many to be only a logical extension.

At the same time, the lack of coordinated planning had produced a set of conflicts between the effects of public sector decision making in different areas which were and are part of the reason for the ineffectiveness of public sector provision. These conflicts, inevitably, show up at local level, and rebound most sharply on the local authorities who have little, and declining, power to resolve them. Hence the battle over the direction of public sector development or decline has been fought out in part as a battle over the powers of local government.

It is the argument of this paper that it is unproductive for those social scientists most concerned with the decline in public services, to attempt to defend public provision by proposing a reversal to the pre-1979 process of public sector economic management. The best defence is to attack the problem at its roots, by arguing for a new and more effective approach. That approach, it is proposed here, must seek to plan the public sector more effectively, treating it as a collection of production activities which still have considerable economic power, and planning them to further a set of aims written in terms of those activities' impact on the operation of the whole economy, nationally and locally.

In other words, public sector planning should start by seeking to coordinate the decisions of that sector in order to produce a specified economic effect. That effect should be specified, not only in terms of the output of each industry or service, but also in terms of their collective external impact on each other and on the private sector.

This paper explores the background to this set of assertions with reference to a single case. It is therefore intended to be a suggestive rather than a definitive argument, a reflection of work in progress. The next few sections discuss public transport planning, with particular reference to London. Most of the material for the paper is drawn from the debate about the proper criteria for transport planning which went on within the Greater London Council between 1981 and 1986.

Transport planning: the issues

The Livingstone administration at the GLC was responsible for public transport in London from the 1981 elections until July 1984, when the government legislated to remove London Transport from GLC control as a preparation for abolition of the Council. At the same time, the Council was the traffic authority for London, and directly responsible for the major roads through the capital except for a number of trunk roads under Department of Transport control. It was also the political authority responsible for coordinating transport policy for the capital[3].

During the life of the administration its transport policy seemed to be rarely out of the newspapers. The most public battles were over public transport fares, and the 'ban' on large lorries from the city at nights and weekends. Many other aspects of the policies were also widely discussed in the local media: the argument over the widely-disliked pay-as-you-enter buses; the fate of the big bus and rail engineering works in West London; the opposition to major road schemes; the measures to improve conditions for cyclists; the bus lanes; the research on the transport needs of women; the list could go on and on.

Behind the scenes, within the Council and between the Council, London Transport and the government, these public battles over specific policies stimulated a different though closely related debate. This debate centred on some of the general issues those policy battles raised about the proper criteria for planning transport. It is some of those general issues that are discussed briefly here.

These general issues can be classified for our purposes here into three groups. First, there was a set of issues about serving need and predicting demand: how in other words London Transport, and the road planners, understood their markets. Second, there were some interrelated arguments about the employment and industrial policies pursued by London Transport. And third, there was a series of disagreements about the impact of transport provision on changes in private sector activity.

All three of these issues involved a sharp difference of opinion on one central point: should transport provision be used as a tool of urban employment policy in London? To many transport planners, the suggestion that it should so be used was heresy. The employment officers, however, observed that the revenue spending alone on London Transport formed a quarter of the GLC's revenue budget in 1984/5, far outweighing the £30 million available to fund the Greater London Enterprise Board; and that the fifty eight thousand staff employed by London Transport outnumbered the twenty one thousand directly employed by the GLC. Given the priority put by the administration on employment generation, the employment officers therefore argued that the employment and general economic impact of the transport spending should be a criterion for its allocation. A great deal of the detailed argument which followed centred on whether the GLC could legally at that time incorporate employment criteria into transport planning; those arguments are ignored here. The following sections briefly set out the policy and research content of the debate, focussing on the three sets of issues listed above.

Services, need and demand

How should a public transport authority decide how many services, and which, should be run? The question has a decidedly anachronistic air, in most parts of the country, given that outside London public authorities have largely lost that power[4]. In London, however, deregulation is still in the wings, and London Regional Transport, the government's creation in 1984, still has the power to license bus routes, the government having been wary of the impact of deregulation in London's dense traffic network. And in the early 1980s, this question was the concern of transport authorities throughout the country, including London.

In London decisions on routes and services were made by London Transport – ultimately by its Board, or Executive – with the GLC having the duty to specify policy guidelines for the organization. The overall level of services run was determined more directly by the GLC, since the level of subsidy was set by the Council, and in turn was calculated to support a given service. Up to the arrival of the Livingstone administration, joint work by the GLC and London Transport planners, on generally agreed assumptions, had determined the proposals for funding, with conflict emerging from time to time over the level of subsidy the politicians were prepared to fund.

The implied, though rather unstable, consensus on planning assumptions broke down after 1981. The new administration came in pledged to lower fares, and raise services: this had been by far their most popular election plank. The history of the battles through the courts over 'Fares Fair' are not part of this paper[5]. The need however to defend the policy in court, and to assess its implications for insertion into the transport planning process, led to two sets of interesting disagreements over transport policy criteria. The first was over the determinants of the total level of demand for services, and the level of services justified by that demand. The second was over the kind of services run, and therefore, of course, the demand for individual services.

To take the determinants of the level of demand first, the central subject of debate was the deeply pessimistic demand model for public transport in London which the transport planners used as a basis for their projections. Briefly, this model took as its database the sharp decline which public transport provision and use had suffered in London since the early 1950s, and predicted on the basis of this history a continued, inexorable 'underlying decline' of about 2 per cent a year in the 1980s, before any changes in policy. While the model allowed that reductions in service levels reduced demand, as did higher fares, it implied that services would have to go on getting better, and fares lower, and therefore subsidies higher were demand to be kept at the same level.

The new generation of GLC officers, hired by the new administration - plus some critics already in post, stimulated by the new administration to move from passive sniping to active proposals for alternatives - cheerfully refused to accept this conclusion on the basis of the evidence offered. They argued that the demand model was misleading. The unexplained time trend, they said, made no conceptual sense: how could public transport demand sink towards zero, in a city where there was not enough room on the roads for the 17 per cent of commuters who did come in by car?

Instead, the critics argued that the apparent trend was largely a proxy for other factors, notably for London Transport's own reaction function, which were creating a downward spiral. London Transport had been, in their own words, matching services to demand over time, by lowering services each time demand fell. At some periods they had failed to recruit sufficient bus workers, thus driving people away from bus services which were increasingly unreliable, an unreliability reinforced by problems of bus maintenance. Through lack of investment London Transport had also effectively been discouraging people from using an increasingly dirty and depressing underground system. Finally, the ticket system was a positive discouragement for travellers wanting to use the public transport system for a range of purposes, as it forced people to pay more if they switched between bus and tube.

Not all these policies had been chosen by London Transport alone. The GLC had had overall control throughout the 1970s, and central government policies, from incomes policy to rules for access to bus purchase grants had played their role[6]. But the implication was that policy, not 'underlying decline', had played the largest role in reducing public transport demand. Based on these argument, the new officers and allies predicted a large increase in use of the system, as a result of fares reform, more investment and more services. The established transport planners predicted a small response, not justifying the cost.

The figures are now in to assess the balance of this argument, and they are quite unequivocally against the old transport planning presumptions. As a result of the lower fares, and the 'Travelcard' (a pass available for bus and tube), introduced in May 1983, plus new investment in the Underground and higher services on buses and tubes, passenger numbers using the system have shot up, pushing up London Transport/LRT revenues, and confounding even the optimists! By mid-1986, bus use had gone up 19 per cent and travel on the tube had risen an astonishing 53 per cent. Some of this was the result of people switching from bus to underground, when there was no longer a penalty on switching, which makes the rise in bus use even more striking. One hears no longer about 'declining underlying demand'.

Looking back on that debate, it is clear that the problem was not merely one of a difference over the specification of an econometric model. Underlying the pessimism of the planners was a long history of largely unexplored assumptions about who uses public transport and why. These assumptions formed an interlocking pattern, difficult to break into.

Briefly, the three most important assumptions were the following. First, transport planning practice took the current and historical usage of the transport system as a reliable guide for current service planning: very few studies had ever been done of the scope for reorganizing routes and provision to provide better for need, or for demand unexpressed because unserved. Second, there was the view that public transport was an inferior mode of transport to the car, so that anyone who could acquire access to a car would use it by preference wherever possible. This implied that while rush hour travel by public transport might be expected to hold up quite well, (commuters having little choice), off-peak public transport was a doomed market. And third, while most transport planners knew quite well that transport investments and decisions - a new railway, a new bus route, loss of an old one, a new road - had a major impact on where people chose or were forced to live and work, they regarded that effect as too difficult to take into account in making decisions. Such an attitude was the equivalent of assuming away such effects, and thereby misunderstanding the market for transport by leaving out of account the ways in which transport investment and transport planning decisions acted to shape and reshape the market itself.

One implication of this self-sustaining net of assumptions was that it was impossible to tell to what extent the public transport system provided for need. A pioneering survey of Women and Transport, organized and commissioned by the GLC Women's Committee, raised a whole series of issues not generally regarded as central to the transport planning process[7]. It also made clear how omitting women's transport need created misunderstanding of the development of the transport market. Women, the survey demonstrated, depended more heavily than men on a service which decreasingly met their needs. The women notably emphasized safety and convenience of access as important factors in determining their bus use, especially disliking the more inconvenient pay-as-you-enter buses, and the reductions in staff on bus and underground. The women needed to make short local journeys, including a lot of off-peak travel for part-time work and other responsibilities, but fares and service structures favoured the longer journeys to work made predominantly by men.

Other less detailed observations than this survey also suggested strongly that needs for transport might be increasingly unmet, especially for low-income Londoners. For example, London had seen a centralization of services - both public and private - over the 1960s and 1970s: previously dispersed shops, schools, hospitals were enlarged and reduced in number, or cut altogether; in the 1980s, the trend worsened. But public transport had not changed sufficiently in cost and scope to allow people to reach these centralized services without penalty. There was no mechanism for reliably coordinating changes in public sector provision with changes in public transport needed to support them, this depending on *ad hoc* pressure channelled through local authorities. And it seemed likely that people in some areas were becoming increasingly cut off, especially as unemployment developed. Once people are unemployed, in a city as large as London, the cost of public transport can very sharply affect the standard of living they can manage on their incomes.

The evidence on unmet need the GLC did collect was sufficient to justify a detailed study into transport need in one area with poor transport. The methodological difficulty with such a study was that, if people on low incomes are faced with poor public transport, then this can have the effect of narrowing their long term horizons and hopes. That in turn means that they do not need to travel (for work, to socialize) which they might otherwise have developed. The study therefore intended to examine not only expressed need, but also the impact of poor transport on people's longer term lives. Interestingly perhaps, this is one small area of spending which the Department of the Environment would not agree to sanction, after it acquired powers over Council spending in 1985.

This lack of investigation of need for transport constituted in part a lack of good market research, and in part an unwillingness to consider transport as a provision for need (especially for those on low incomes) as well as a provision for demand. Both of these failings were a source of public dissatisfaction with the system. It became clear that there needed to be more organized forms of public pressure on the transport system to reorganize routes and provision. While the GLC funded a much more critical passenger committee than had previously been seen, it had got little further with developing passenger involvement before it lost control of London Transport. But it is clear that, while good market research is important, if a public service is to provide for need, and influence income distribution, then it also requires organized forms of public pressure and participation in planning.

Management and employment

Associated with the philosophy of decline, and misperception of markets, just described, was another set of problems for public transport policy: the issues of management criteria for investment, internal organization and employment policy. The management of public transport in London appeared to the new GLC employment officers to have become increasingly inward looking and problematic over the 1960s and 1970s. The debate which followed could be summarized as one between, on the one hand, a management philosophy based on the least cost management of a declining service, and on the other, a possible alternative involving active development of a potentially growing public sector industry.

This issue of management philosophy was brought forward most sharply over the question of bus and rail engineering policy[8]. London Transport had three major engineering works in the early 1980s. Since 1984, one has now been closed, and one largely dismantled, leaving only a much smaller engineering shop. The proposals for contraction of the works first came to the Livingstone administration in 1983, facing the GLC with sharp contradictions: the Council was at the same time trying to save and develop employment in London, and in danger of destroying twenty five thousand skilled and semi-skilled engineering jobs under its own control.

When the Council investigated the proposals, it found that the proposals for closure of Aldenham bus works, and contraction of the other works were not new. They had been put forward and withdrawn before, in the early 1970s. Their return represented, it can be argued, the end result of a philosophy of engineering management which had developed within London Transport over thirty years, in a progression probably far from unique in the public sector.

Post-war London Transport engineering philosophy had initially been based in a strong involvement by their own design team in the design and construction of the buses run by the organization. The philosophy had included a maintenance policy of periodic overhaul for both buses and trains, which had given the organization a substantial level of control over the length of life of their stock. The engineering works, notably the rail works, had taken in outside orders to supplement in-house work. And the works had had good apprenticeship schemes, and a commitment to in-house maintenance integrated with management of services.

Over the post-war years, London Transport had progressively moved away from this starting point. They reduced their involvement in bus design, buying 'off the peg' and less easily maintainable vehicles. The seeking of outside work seemed to decline: certainly outside work was not seen as a potential response to over capacity. By the early 1980s, and under pressure from a government-ordered Monopolies and Mergers Commission investigation into the bus works[9], this general move had coalesced into a series of more detailed proposals. These included: fragmentation of management of engineering into a number of profit centres separate from service provision; contracting-out of a substantial part of the engineering overhaul work; resultant closure of a large part of the works, and of course very sharp decrease in apprenticeships.

This faced the GLC with a serious policy problem, which suggested its own potential solution. The North West of London, where the bus and rail works were located, had experienced a huge loss in engineering jobs in the early 1980s. To illustrate the scale of the problem: by 1983, London Transport apprenticeships had come to represent over half of all the engineering apprenticeships remaining in the area. If the Council agreed to the closure of these works, it would practically finish London's vehicle engineering industry: most of the contracted out work would have to be driven up and down to the Midlands. The question was, should the Council bow to this logic of the private market in the public sector? Or was there an economic case for resistance?

Investigating this issue, the GLC, the trade unions and the consultants the GLC hired to help, concluded that there was a viable alternative to this agenda of contraction and privatization of the engineering services. The alternative agenda would begin by rejecting the short-term perspective of the management proposals. The contracting out proposals were justified by the management on cost cutting terms, without in the Council's view[10] sufficient study of the long-term revenue and cost implications. One outside management consultant was led to comment that this was hardly satisfactory: on cost grounds alone, the best solution would be to cease to provide transport services[11]! The problems for service reliability that might be caused by dispersing maintenance among many private suppliers were in the Council's view underestimated[12].

There were reasons, too, for thinking that the cost advantages of contracting-out might have been overestimated. London Transport's internal cost accounting was poor[13]. The Council took the view, on the basis of work done by the trade unionists on checking contractors' work, that the management were taking private sector initial pricing and quality estimates too much at face value. By contracting out some work, they were likely to start a 'cascade' of subcontracting – where shifting the internal overheads onto fewer activities in turn made them vulnerable to contracting-out – and thereby likely to end up depending on a whole range of subcontractors outside London for overhaul. Or they might end by not doing regular overhaul at all[14].

An alternative agenda would seek to reverse this spiral. By looking to the longer term, (in the manner of good corporate management), it would try to spread the engineering overheads by looking for new work, while also developing the works to service a changing transport system. Research demonstrated that there was a need for vehicles better adapted to London's transport needs, and that the economics of bus building did not exclude design and building being done at least partly in the works.[15] The Greater London Enterprise Board started looking for new work for the works, and the council funded market research into opportunities for taking in outside maintenance. It became clear that both were viable strategies: while the formation of LRT put an end by law to the attempts to develop new production work, by the time Aldenham works was closed by the LRT Board, its management, pressured by the unions, had found a substantial and increasing market for outside maintenance work for the works.[16]

This strategy would imply, therefore, taking a more entrepreneurial attitude to the use of the works capacity in a recession. It would imply treating, so far as possible, the works as a resource for London and its labour as far as possible as a fixed cost in the recession: seeking to develop the assets, not to make them redundant., That in turn might have involved some direct funding of apprenticeships there, as a contribution to London training efforts, including changing and upgrading the kind of training done, (to include, for example, new electronics skills). And a background of an expanding and changing public transport system would have relied on, and forced changes in, the maintenance practices.

It was clear from research done that this was a viable alternative route for the organization to explore. It was largely blocked by government transport policy. Standing back from the story now, the debate makes clear that the last GLC administration began in 1981 with a policy for public transport services, but no clear industrial policy to determine the management strategy to be applied by the organization as a whole. That lack meant that it was ill prepared to face other problems in addition to the engineering works: the issue of one-person operation of buses and tubes, for example, or internal equal opportunities policies, or industrial democracy and the role of unions in the organization. One of the most striking features of the alternative approach just set out was the extent to which it was developed through collaboration between the unions and the Council; this in itself raised a whole series of important issues about how to formulate management strategy for the public sector[17]. By the time the Council began to get a grip on all these issues, it was losing control of London Transport to the government.

This part of the story of London's transport planning,

too, suggests some general lessons. Too often, political debate on management strategy for nationalized industries and services is seen as undesirable interference. To accept that view meant accepting that the public transport system in London, including its skilled engineering capacity, should be run down. The arguments for looking for an alternative approach began from the wider interests of the London economy. Once you begin from that point of view, then the internal management strategy of public sector services and industries becomes a legitimate concern of wider economic strategy making: a legitimate part of economic planning of the public sector.

Transport and the private market

Economic historians and geographers both give considerable importance to transport investment and service provision, among the forces which determine the location and scope of economic activity. From the opening up of areas by railways in the nineteenth century, through the spreading of economic activity along (some) roads since the war, to the draining of economic activity out of other areas when roads were built, to the impact of public transport accessibility on house prices in big cities today, it has been clear that transport decisions are one force determining the pattern and profits of private sector activity.

But oddly, when one turns to transport planning, the argument is in practice reversed. The author of this paper has sat in meetings and listened to high level transport planners argue that because the impact of transport on private sector activity (and therefore employment) is difficult to identify, it should therefore be omitted from the calculations. Transport planning should, it is thus argued, serve the existing patterns of demand, derived from existing patterns of activity, not lead that demand by creating new private market opportunities, and that is in practice how the models are generally constructed. There have been exceptions; for example Docklands Light Railway was partly justified on the basis of its employment generating capacity; but they are relatively rare[18].

One of the many evident problems with this general view is that it has as its consequence, not that transport decisions do not continue to influence private market activity, but they generally do so in an unstudied and unregulated way. To give one example: one effect of the decline in industrial employment in the 1970s was that, in response to firm closure, a number of industrial estates in London lost their bus services. This effectively put a block on redevelopment on a piecemeal basis. It was easily possible to find East London employers in the early 1980s, when London unemployment was rising towards half a million, who could not get lower paid workers because of lack of public transport to their areas[19].

This section describes briefly a more detailed example of the same phenomenon: public transport decisions apparently blocking the development of employment and economic activity in areas where planners and economic development officers were trying to promote it. The data are taken from an unpublished study of travel and transport to a number of London subsidiary town centres over thirty years[20].

These town centres - Lewisham and Stratford in East London are the examples used here - were areas with newly redeveloped commercial centres, where shopping and public services were increasingly concentrated. GLC researchers compared travel patterns (including private cars) and transport provision to these centres, over thirty years, and some interesting results emerged.

First, some very brief background. In the area around these two town centres, car ownership was low (half the households had no car in Lewisham town centre area, and 60 per cent had none in Stratford); both have high levels of urban poverty and are within areas that lost employment fast in the 1970s. Unemployment in 1981 in the area of the boroughs around the town centres[21] was 13 per cent for men in Lewisham and 16 per cent in Stratford. Both town centres were envisaged by planners as providing sources of future jobs, especially in commerce and services.

The most striking results of the research were as follows. Lewisham, the area which had stood up the better to recession, had seen, after a drop in the 1960s, a relatively constant number of journeys to work in the 1970s: a somewhat declining proportion by public transport; an only slightly rising number by private car, and a sharp increase in arrival on feet or bicycles. But, quite contrary to public transport service planners' assumptions, non-work journeys had shot up (by almost 50 per cent in the 1970s), and of this increase half the additional journeys were by bus, especially for shopping.

The same pattern reappears in Stratford, only more sharply given the poverty of the area. Total journeys to work in Stratford fell drastically (by 35 per cent) in the 1970s. Bus and car use for going to work therefore fell. But again, non-work travel to the city centre, especially for shopping rose fast in the 1970s. Total non-work trips by bus rose 64 per cent, while non-work car use fell against the national and London trend.

Much of this non-work travel is of course off-peak: not at 9.00 and 5.00, but during the day. In both areas, constant or rising overall bus use was met by declining provision of buses. Both rush hour and off-peak bus services have been heavily cut, but the scale of the off-peak cuts in the face of rising non-work bus use is particularly striking. Lewisham saw sharp cuts in bus provision in the 1960s and 1970s, throughout the week: the cuts on Saturday, the busiest shopping day, were particularly striking. In Stratford, a huge rise in bus use for non-work activity has been met by only a very slight rise in bus provision on weekdays, and (again) a further decline on Saturdays. (Four tables in an

Appendix summarize the data on which these assertions about bus use and provision are based.)

Now, one person's non-work shopping trip helps support another person's shop assistant pay packet. The data (including data on train use not presented here, which reinforces the picture) suggest, at the very least, that transport policy has for a long time been actively undermining local efforts to provide public infrastructure of other types in order to encourage private activity. This tentative conclusion is reinforced by surveys of employers' and employees' opinions [22]: the drop in buses and trains has made the services unreliable, so that employees lost large numbers of working hours because of public transport problems. And poor route planning and provision effectively cut off Lewisham especially from easy access by people eg from Southwark seeking lower paid jobs.

Town centre developments within a dense city must rely on public transport: road building and parking cannot cope; those employed, especially the women, often cannot afford cars; and in Stratford, the large roads have made the environment unpleasant, not brought an increase in car use, and made parts of the area at the edges of the large roads very inaccessible to potential workers. Both centres depend for their commercial viability on good bus services which they do not have. Both have a problem recruiting and keeping lower paid white collar staff, especially women, in areas of high unemployment, a problem worsened, at least, by the lack of satisfactory bus connections from the inner city labour market surrounding them. And both centres are therefore suffering commercially from the inertia and misperceptions of bus planning.

All these conclusions, like the rest of this paper, are tentative. But they do illustrate the central point of this section: that transport policy actively influences overall economic development in, for example, London. The example illustrates again how one kind of public sector activity - in this case encouraging commercial centre development - can be partly frustrated by problems with another. There is beginning to be some research on these issues just at the moment when, in transport and in other areas, local authorities face greatly decreased powers. There is no doubt that the external impact of public investment on the private market is difficult to establish: but it can and should be researched, and the research incorporated into an effort to improve public sector planning.

Conclusion: leading or following the market?

One might summarize the above discussion as follows. In a number of ways, transport planning has misunderstood the transport market, and misunderstood or ignored transport's wider market impact. Part of the reason has been an inward looking and pessimistic set of planning principles and assumptions for public transport. Part of the result has been a series of conflicts with other public sector policies, and a decline in the public transport industry, to the detriment of the London economy. The future appears to hold more of the same, but worse.

But, the above argument further implies, this process is not inevitable, though it is reinforced by the extent to which the current policies appear to be reacting to past problems - in service provision - while building on past assumptions - in institutional terms. There are in fact two alternative approaches open to the management and development of the (substantial) remains of the public sector.

The public sector's investment and production activities have, however they are organized, a major impact on the operation of the private market and the development of the local and national economy. The current approach is to import into this public sector as many market-like criteria and market pressures as possible: to attempt (though it will not wholly work) to let the private lead the public. The alternative is to reverse the chain of thought, and to coordinate public production as consciously as possible to pressure the private market to develop in ways more socially and economically desirable. That would certainly not wholly work either. But in dense urban areas especially, where the externalities of private activity are so drastic in their effects, and the network of public infrastructure so important in modifying and directing those effects, the outcome would be greatly to be preferred.

In transport in London, such an alternative approach might imply, for example, consciously making use of transport's capacity to lead the private market. It might mean more tubes and buses, lower fares, absence of encouragement to car use (of the kind implied by the current huge subsidy for company cars), conscious planning of transport to link labour market and employment centres, especially within the inner city, better coordination of transport provision with other public service provision, and proper investigation of need and the income distribution effects of transport policies. It might imply integrated planning of services and maintenance, an industrial policy favouring industrial and labour force development, industrial democracy within public transport, and popular involvement in service planning.

More generally, if we are to stop acquiescing in the private market setting the terms of public sector activity, then such a major shift in perspective is required. Public sector activity, including service provision, has to be treated as production and investment, not just as 'spending'[23]. Mechanisms have to be found to overcome the problems of public sector performance which are not market solutions: they certainly have to lie in the direction of increased democratic and public pressure, and more involvement of the workforce in the development of their own industries and services. Such mechanisms can lead to the better serving of public sector markets: but those markets need redefining to have a clearer element of need and long term development. And ways have to be found to coordinate public sector activity much better in the pursuit of more desirable public and private sector economic outcomes. This involves bringing wider economic considerations into the planning of individual public sector activities: using those activities as tools of economic policy.

Finally let me return to my comments at the beginning. This paper is a speculative piece, based almost entirely on one case. Each public sector activity has some different pressures and problems. Nevertheless, general knowledge suggests, if only in areas where other public sector activities touch the transport sector, that some of the issues outlined are far from confined to transport. The public sector could contribute much more effectively to economic regeneration, but it needs to be planned more effectively, in the sense defined above, and used more effectively to further planned ends.

Lewisham and Stratford Town Centres: Transport and Employment
Data

TABLE 1: Journeys by bus to Lewisham town centre, 1962-1981

	Work	Shopping	Other non-work
1962	9780	10418	3725
1971	7377	10619	5613
1981	4400	15004	3797

Source: London Traffic Survey 1962, Greater London Transportation Surveys
1971, 1981

TABLE 2: Percentage change in buses/hour arriving in Lewisham
centre, 1962-1981

	1962-1971	1971-1981
Weekday peak	- 7%	-28%
Weekday between peaks	-14%	- 9%
Weekday evenings	-21%	- 8%
Saturdays	-14%	-11%
Sundays	-42%	+ 1%

Source: London Transport bus timetables

TABLE 3: Journeys by bus to Stratford town centre 1962-1981

	Work	Shopping	Other non-work
1962	19598	1220	5785
1971	11796	1964	3291
1981	7471	9697	3929

Source: As Table 1

TABLE 4: Stratford: Percentage changes in buses/hour arriving

	1962-1971	1971-1981
Weekday peak	-36%	-15%
Weekday between peaks	-28%	+ 1%
Weekday evenings	-20%	-14%
Saturday	-39%	- 2%
Sunday	-42%	+ 8%

Source: As Table 2

NOTE

This paper is a rewritten version of a talk given at the Open University's Conference on Local Economic Strategies in December 1986.[1] As such, it is a speculative piece, rather than a detailed research paper. It draws on the author's experience of working on the employment impact of the Greater London Council's transport policies[2], and its aim is to contribute to reflection on an agenda for research and rethinking about the economics and politics of planning the public sector.

Footnotes

[1] Conference on Local Economic Strategies, Parsifal College, December 17/18 1986. The author would like to thank the conference participants for their comments on this paper, which remains however the author's responsibility.

[2] The views in this paper are the views of the author, and not those of the Council except where explicitly stated. The work on transport planning on which it draws owes a very great deal to the author's colleagues at the GLC, especially Dick Hallé and Jane Smith. My thanks to them both; where their written work is drawn on it is cited below, but they bear no responsibility for the use I have made of it here. The views and policies of the Council towards the employment impact of public transport are set out in The London Industrial Strategy, GLC 1985, in the chapter on Public Transport. A later chapter published separately entitled Freight and Roads, GLC 1986, sets out the employment aspects of roads-related policies.

(3) The Council was responsible for publishing three year forward plans for London's tansport: these were contained in the GLC's annual <u>Transport Policies and Programmes</u>.

(4) The Buses Act, 1986, deregulated public bus transport throughout the country with the exception of London.

(5) 'Fares Fair' was the name given by the GLC to their policy of lower fares, implemented after the 1981 election, challenged in the courts and defeated in the House of Lords in 1982. The story and its aftermath in terms of new fares policies and their impact is briefly told in <u>The London Industrial Strategy</u> *op cit* and in 'Public Transport Engineering: The GLC and the Transport Unions', chapter in <u>A Taste of Power: The Politics of Local Economics</u> (eds) M Mackintosh and H Wainwright, Verso (forthcoming) 1987.

(6) New Bus Grants, when introduced, were tied to purchase of a particular type of bus. The question of bus design and reliability, and bus policy more generally, is discussed in an accessible format in <u>London's Buses: Back on the Road,</u> GLC 1985. This and other GLC publications are available from the London Strategic Policy Unit, (20 Vauxhall Bridge Road, London SW1).

(7) <u>Women on the Move</u> GLC Survey on Women and Transport, GLC 1985 and 1986 (ten pamphlets).

(8) See <u>London Industrial Strategy</u> *op cit* and 'Public Transport Engineering' *op cit*.

(9) <u>London Transport Executive. A report on the arrangements made by the Executive for the maintenance of buses and</u>

coaches Monopolies and Mergers Commission, HMSO, cmnd 9133, February 1984.

(10) The Council's view on these matters is set out in a committee paper entitled, 'London Transport: Policy Guidelines on Subcontracting and Associated Internal Reorganization', approved by the Industry and Employment and Transport Committees, GLC 1984.

(11) The comment is contained in a consultancy report to the GLC, reviewing London Transport management's proposals for Action rail works.

(12) 'London Transport: Policy Guidelines' *op cit*. The report points out that London Transport was ignoring warnings from other transport operators about unreliability of service caused by sub-contracting maintenance.

(13) The Monopolies and Mergers Commission had pointed to problems in internal cost control; London Transport's white collar staff, investigating the problem for the union side during the negotiations about subcontracting, also identified problems in determining costs. See 'Public Transport Engineering' *op cit*.

(14) This is in fact the direction which practice has now taken at London Regional Transport.

(15) This work was undertaken partly by consultants, partly by the GLC, and partly by the GLEB's London Transport Technology Network, which is still in existence. The research demonstrated that economies of scale in bodybuilding were not such as to exclude bus construction for the London market alone.

(16) I owe this information to Mr Tom Holland, previously working at Aldenham bus works, and now a London regional official of the Transport and General Workers Union.

(17) The working relations between London Transport trade unionists and the Council are discussed in 'Public Transport Engineering' *op cit.*

(18) There has been some research on these effects, and some use of them to justify transport spending. See for example <u>Greater Manchester Rail Strategy Study: The Development Impact</u> Greater Manchester Council December 1984. See also 'The Transport Problems of Inner City Firms: An Approach to Solutions' Patterson, N. and Mackie, A., <u>Working Paper</u> 155, Institute for Transport Studies, University of Leeds, December 1981.

(19) <u>London Industrial Strategy</u> *op cit.*

(20) A work in progress report on this research was presented in 'Employment, Transport Accessibility and Travel in a Sample of London Town Centres and Industrial Areas', Dawson, H., Halle´, D., Mackintosh, M. and Smith, J., paper presented to the GLC's Transport and Employment Conference, June 1985. The data used in the Appendix to this present paper were compiled by Jane Smith and Dick Halle´. None of the other authors of the research paper are responsible for the use I make of the data here.

(21) Analysis was undertaken of a number of wards surrounding the two town centres, within the wider boroughs of Newham and Lewisham.

(22) In particular, this drew on 'The Potential for and Impact of Office Development in the Inner City in London', Damesick, P., <u>Progress in Planning</u>, vol 18, 1982, and 'An

Employment and Journey to Work Survey of Lewisham Town Centre', Davies, K., GLC Technical Note, 1984.

(23) The treatment of public production as 'spending' and the lumping together of investment and revenue under this heading is characteristic of public sector economics texts at present. See for example, <u>Public Sector Economics</u> Brown, C. and Jackson, P., Blackwell, 1986, where public sector investment is rarely differentiated from revenue in the analysis.

4 SOCIAL INVESTMENT IN PRODUCTION
Keith Jefferis & Mike Robinson

Introduction

Intervention by the left involves a change of direction of local economic strategy, towards direct intervention in production. Typically it has attempted more than simply the restoration of profitability to enterprises which face commercial problems. To quite the London Industrial Strategy, 'restructuring for labour' involves 'social' objectives, or, '... not the priorities of the balance sheet, but the provision of work for all who wish it in jobs that are geared to meeting social need' (GLC, 1985a, 18) - with - 'better wages and conditions, greater social control within the enterprise, equal opportunities, and socially useful production' (GLC, 1985a, 38).

This 'economics of labour' (GLC, 1985a, 18) involves intervention in both individual enterprises and in physical and economic infrastructure. Intervention in physical infrastructure has a fairly long history. Sewage and refuse collection; roads and transport; health and education; housing, leisure, and social welfare are all areas where, historically, local authorities have fought for, and eventually won the right of intervention. In a capitalist economy, direct intervention in particular enterprises and the wider economy was a radically new departure. There were few precedents and little practical experience.

If the sphere of production is to be restructured in favour of labour, then clearly the enterprise must be one object of attention; it is here that work takes place and where the quality of work is experienced. While the enterprise is the unit of economic activity, success or failure (by whatever criteria) is also determined by the economic environment, and that environment must be restructured. This paper is concerned largely with the first object: direct intervention at the level of the enterprise. We will try to build on the experience of the GLC. In particular we will be looking at social intervention that involved putting money into firms, which we will term 'social investment'. We will review the criteria of social investment, and relate this to criteria that have been used – and might be used – for 'social return' on 'social investment'.

Both authors are interested in the relation between cooperatives and technology. In particular, how the GLC's investment in technology, cooperatives, and other forms of 'social production' clarified, and opened new options in this area.

We believe that the technology used in production limits the ways in which a cooperative can be organized. There is an *insistent*[1] relationship between the way an organization is controlled, and the forms of technology it has adopted.

Tom Clarke makes the same point in a powerful way:

The form of *technology* adopted by cooperatives will have an important bearing on organization and control. A commercial cooperative normally would install the same least-cost technology as private competitors, almost regardless of the consequences for shopfloor workers. This ignores the fact that industrial technology and production engineering were designed and introduced partly with the aim of restructuring the labour process under capital's control, with the intensification of labour, the imposition of a detailed division of labour, and the adoption of scientific management to discipline labour (Braverman, 1974; Marx, 1976). A cooperative that adopts this form of mass production technology must accept that shopfloor workers will exhibit similar levels of alienation as exist under the same technology in private industry. That the debilitating impact of modern production technology is not more widespread in cooperatives is not the result of an enlightened attitude to the social implications of technology, but simply due to the small size and capital starvation of most cooperatives that prevents them from investing in mass production machinery
(Clarke, 1984).

There is no *a priori* reason to believe that efficiency - ie maximizing the amount of output from a given input to production - can only be achieved with technology developed for capitalist purposes. 'Socialist technology' can be equally as efficient (Gordon, 1976), and have many other benefits for the workers involved. Not surprisingly there is little 'socialist technology' to be had in the Capitalist West. Perhaps part of the Eastern Block's failings in the achievement of democracy can be put down to its replication of western technology. It never really tried to develop an alternative democratic socialist technology. The development of such technology is integral to the economics of labour (Rosenbrock, 1983).

Pioneering work in 'socialist technology' by CAITS and Rosenbrock was enhanced by the GLC's establishment of the London Technology Networks. Their aim was to provide a resource of socially responsible technology. This would be utilized by workers' cooperatives, trade unions, and companies which had been 'intervened in' to move away from the exploitation of capitalist employment.

Investments in technology in cooperatives are linked to the much wider question of the impact of investments amde on social rather than commercial grounds. In the next section, we will look at some of the links and differences between financial and social investment.

Social and financial investment

Conventional financial investment by banks and other institutions is carried out on the basis of minimum risk and maximum profit. Whether loan or equity, an assessment is made of the likely financial returns to be gained from a particular investment before deciding whether or not to proceed. Mainstream financial institutions themselves are of course profit-maximizing enterprises. Their activities are in principle little different to those of any profit-maximizing firms in a capitalist market economy. But banks do occupy a central role in the health or otherwise of the economy given the importance of finance to virtually any other economic activity. Britain has its own particular problems with finance capital (Fine and Harris, 1985). But even without these added difficulties, there are two general consequences of banking activity.

Firstly, it is only financial returns within the enterprise which are relevant to the consideration of an investment. Externalities are not considered, even though their effects are none the less real for the rest of society.

Conventional financial appraisal of the returns from an investment is therefore not a financial appraisal from the point of view of society. The Social Audit has been developed as a means of incorporating some external financial aspects. For instance, it includes the costs of unemployment benefit and other payments to redundant workers when the costs of a factory closure are being considered (Rowthorn and Ward, 1983; Coates, 1981).

The second consequence is that limited financial appraisal, even when qualified by Social Audit, refers to gains and losses which can be quantified financially. Undamaged environments, racial and sexual equality, and healthy people cannot be quantified in this way. Damage and injustice often has cost-based indicators. Positive social, non-financial returns are excluded. This is particularly important in the context of the type of economic intervention that we are concerned with. Investments by local authorities with the aim of 'restructuring for labour' are as much social investments as financial ones. In parallel with the accepted idea of a financial return, we would expect such social investments to generate a social return.

Conventional financial criteria cannot be uncritically applied to the investments made by GLEB and similar bodies in projects with social objectives. Some projects will generate an adequate financial return[2]: 'restructuring for labour' does not *necessarily* mean that an enterprise will not be commercially viable[3].

In many cases, however, investments would not be viable on narrow, commercial terms. Developing equal opportunities and improving the quality of work, perhaps through job rotation and widening the skills of those in low-skilled jobs, will almost certainly require investment of time and money in training activities. The development of an alternative form of technology and labour process within an enterprise, for the benefit of the workforce, is likely to incur a cost in terms of profitability - in the short-term at least.

Such investments would not normally be capable of paying financial returns to a financial investment. They are not, however, like conventionally non-viable investments. They do yield returns, but in other forms. The benefits are of a social and non-financial kind. They are social investments because the provision of capital at sub-commercial rates (perhaps as a grant) represents an investment by society in that project. Here we have productive investment, but instead of financial investment yielding financial returns, we have *social investment* yielding *social returns*.

The idea of social investments is of course central to local economic intervention. What is less developed is the concept of the social return flowing from that investment. In this paper we attempt to develop the idea of the social return, and in particular how consideration of social return can be beneficial to both the enterprise and to society[4].

Our aim here is to move beyond the implicit assumption that any social investment will generate sufficient social returns. We wish to suggest ways in which a formalized social return can be of assistance to both an enterprise and society.

Social objectives and social returns

Social objectives, even realised social objectives, are not social returns. The achievement of social objectives - the result of social investment - may be difficult or inappropriate to quantify.

What counts as the realisation of an objective? A training scheme may reduce the opportunity gaps between the sexes. It is unlikely to eradicate sexism. Some people see the training as progress. Others may see it as a diversion from tackling deeper, root causes. Sexism at work is a complex and diverse problem. Action to change it can be similarly complex and diverse. Training is somewhat uni-dimensional in this context. But it is also progress. The issue is 'fuzzy' simply because progress may be amde, but it cannot be counted on a uni-dimensional scale. The enterprise has conformed with the criteria of investment. It has taken steaps to combat sexism. But we cannot *count* how much closer it is to the objective.

Even in cases where there is monitoring, where some quantification is possible, it may not be possible to establish causality. It may not be possible to 'prove' that local authority investment increased opportunity for women. A case can always be made that this would have happened anyway, or would have happened under other pressures.

A social return does not have this problematic quality. It is agreed that something will be given back to the investor. We do not have to worry about causality. We merely have to see whether the investor gets something back or not. Objectives may or may not be returnable in this sense. Usually they are not. Objectives are by their nature complex, diverse, and 'fuzzy'. A return is much more straightforward. The investors either get it back or they do not.

To put it in another way, social objectives are difficult or impossible to quantify *because* they are seen from several perspectives. For instance, there will usually be many groups with a strong interest in an equal opportunities policy. This objective will have different but overlapping meanings to white men, to women, to black people, to disabled people, and to management within a company, to the investor, and to activist groups outside the company. A social return on the other hand is defined solely from the perspective of the investing authority. Unlike a social objective, it is 'what it gets back'. It should function to strengthen the investing authority in the same way that financial returns strengthen a bank.

But why is it important to define return - as something that comes back - and to distinguish it from objective?

Fundamentally, it is because we are concerned with more than the progress of the individual enterprise. We are equally concerned with the investing authority. The *investment* enhances the viability of the enterprise. The *objectives* affect the enterprise, but also reverberate - ripple out - into much wider social consequences. The *return* enhances the ability of the investing authority to grow and extend its role.

Monitoring objectives is a necessary part of the authority's function. But this is like financial monitoring. It should be practical and limited. Objectives are 'fuzzy' and complex; are a process not an object. The investing authority can spend too much time chasing them in their fine and elusive detail. In doing this it neglects its own real function. This is a consequence of the mistaken belief that objectives can be returns.

This is the question of context. The investment is localized to the enterprise. The objectives take a broad social context. The return should be localized to the investing authority. The return develops the authority's ability to make further investment and other interventions. As we said earlier, this is a similar function to the financial return to a bank.

So the return strengthens the investor as a meta-system - an organization that functions at a different level to the 'assisted' enterprise[5]. A major role of the meta-system is the allocation of social resources - just as banks reallocate capital. Returns from the enterprise(s) are a necessary form of feedback if the allocation of 'social capital' is to be practically engaged with social process, and responsive to real needs. To labour(!) the point: objectives are not returns by nature or by context, and monitoring cannot make them so. But the authority needs the returns just as the enterprise needs the investment.

If we look at the historical record of the GLC and GLEB, in terms of investment in particular enterprises, we can find a lot of evidence of negotiation on social objectives. We can also find a lot of agreements on well-defined economic returns. With the benefit of hindsight, we can say that social returns were less well defined.

Social character of investments

Part of the impact of social policies is felt within the enterprise, directly by the workers involved. But restructuring for labour is not limited to this, it is also about changing external social processes. Improving the quality of work for individual workers is important, but one of the benefits of this should be to provide a resource which other workers can draw upon in attempting to achieve the same objectives. In this way social benefits can be extended as widely as possible. Perhaps this idea is best envisaged as 'social accumulation' as the product of social investment.

The ways in which social benefits can be generalized will vary, depending on the process involved. In this paper we are concentrating in particular upon the development of technology. If a local authority invests in a firm to enable it to develop such technology further, how exactly would this take place, and what can it expect in return? The actual content of the social return, or 'return contract' back into the community which would be required by a local authority is something which would need to be agreed between the authority and the workforce, via trade union representatives. In the case of technology, we envisage a local authority requiring an assisted enterprise to produce a report (at the very least) on its experience of the implementation of technology.

Let us think back to what the aim of this policy is. Broadly, it is to change work processes to increase the opportunities for workers to control their own jobs. But while the appropriate technology is a necessary condition for this to take place, it may not be sufficient. The internal structure is likely to change if a different form of technology is introduced, but it may not change sufficiently for workers to be able to exploit the full potential of this technology. Particularly in companies which remain capitalist controlled, or which are perhaps cooperatives 'rescued' from bankrupt firms, old hierarchical structures are likely to remain.

However, the enterprises we are concerned with are likely to at least have the seeds of a democratic structure, whether as cooperatives or as capitalist companies where an enterprise plan has been developed with TU input. What is attractive about the social return is that it can be used to build upon and strengthen this further.

These changes may not be most effectively achieved by direct means - ie the imposition of new organizational structures from outside. We will argue later that the indirect incentives of a 'return contract' may be more effective in stimulating the emergence of such structures from within the workforce. On positive effect is that it would provide an incentive for management to consult the workforce and utilize their ingenuity in developing the technology. It would thus strengthen the input of the workforce into the management role, and help develop new democratic structures. Combined with other forms of 'return contract' monitoring, such as for equal opportunities, such developments should be appropriate to both the workers in the specific enterprise and the wider social requirements of the restructuring process. A second effect is that the benefits of workers' experience would be available for further application; a form of social accumulation which would contribute to the building up of a resource bank.

JLD Limited

Let us illustrate these ideas with an example. It is fictitious but it is informed by the experience of the GLC with industrial intervention, and by the rescue cooperatives of the last Labour Government.

We have a situation where a factory, JLD Limited, employing five hundred workers is threatened with closure. A multinational is rationalizing, and moving its main operations out of the United Kingdom. There is a market for the products, but the existing machines are outdated. Some of them are obsolete. Investment is needed for job preservation. Investment is needed in new technology so the enterprise can remain viable. In the course of negotiation it is discovered that there is vast scope for improvement in equal opportunities, and in working conditions and processes. Pay is not too bad - this was why the multinational started to move out in the first place - but there is still scope for improvement.

The workforce has approved the shop stewards' motion that JLD should be legally restructured as a cooperative. Let us now assume the unrealistic. Ther is no problem in providing adequate cash investment. Nor, in this scenario, has there been much trouble in agreeing the social as well as the economic objectives.

It is decided that a major investment should be made in technology. Should we consider this as an economic or as a social investment? If we consider it as an economic investment, then we only need to define the economic return: repayment period; repayment levels; interest, and so on. If it is a social investment, how does it relate to equal opportunities? To socially useful products? To humanizing technology? And so on. Investment in technology does not, *per se*, stimulate these processes - although it may facilitate them. *Therefore we need to define a social return* that is distinct from the social objectives.

Economic investment may, and often does have general economic objectives - but it also has well defined economic returns. We need to establish a similar clarity of investment, objectives, and returns in the social sphere. Let us return to our example.

JLD has an internal momentum. It has a history of strong unionization. The workforce has historically demonstrated its ability to resist management demands. This is reflected in pay and in the strong union structure. JLD is weak in the area of equal opportunities. Ethnic minorities are significantly under-represented. No skilled jobs are held by women - or rather, no jobs defined as skilled by status and pay are held by women. On top of this the quality of work is poor. A lot of it is repetitive and boring.

The creativity of the workforce has been directed to union organization, to economic gain, and to the amelioration of the worst of the production conditions. Unofficial tea breaks are institutionalized. Machine breakdown (or not) is under the control of operatives rather than supervisors.

Self-management, the adoption of a legal cooperative form, is unlikely to change this combination of features that we term internal momentum. An attempt to impose changes in areas such as work process and equal opportunities would be inappropriate when we are dealing with a cooperative. Even if this were ignored, or an agreement reached that was *seen* as imposed, this would be likely to reactivate the demonstrated ability of the workforce to resist change.

Thus there are social objectives, and they may be criteria of investment, but they cannot be *conditions* of investment, not more importantly are they the *objects* of investment. The major object of the investment will be, as we have said already, technology. How can these other aspects be integrated?

Using our analogy we need to look for a 'something' that can cross the boundaries of the organization; that can be well defined and subject to agreement; and can serve as an input to the 'meta-system'.

Upgrading the technology at JLD will be considered to be a social investment. The social objectives will be JLD's long-term viability; equal opportunities approached via training; collective control in the cooperative form; and more human work conditions. There is also an objective of commitment - 'engaging all the intelligence, all the inventive power, all the wit and insight' (GLC, 1983, 26) in the enterprise.

This 'intelligence and inventive power', rather like 'peace' is something everybody is in favour of. In practice, even in Workers' States, the response to specific acts of creativity can be very negative. Tom Clarke puts his finger on the 'stultifying work tasks' that can either undermine cooperatives or lead to unexpected innovations.

... both at Mondragon, and at at least one of the large scale cooperatives in Britain (KME), the retention of a detailed division of labour was a source of great disaffection among workers (Eaton, 1979; Clarke, 1978). It is difficult for cooperative workers to feel they are engaging in a great cooperative experiment when their sole cooperative duty is to make several thousand spot welds each day.
(Clarke, 1984, 110)

But what is the usual response to creativity? Here are two striking examples, one from Britain, the other from Cuba.

Night workers at a British Leyland paint shop who were found to be asleep during a spot check may face disciplinary action for an alleged breach of safety regulations.

The fourteen men in Block 38a at the Range Rover plant in Solihull, Birmingham, devised a method of completing their workload halfway through their shift so they could spend the remainder of their time asleep ...

Management made a spot check at 4 am on Friday when most of the workers were found sleeping in the locker room. The conveyor track was switched off.

The men are expected to be called before management today. They will be given the opportunity of having representatives of the Transport and General Workers Union present at the hearing. Disciplinary action could result in suspension or even dismissal.

BL stressed that the men had been keeping to their work schedules and turning in work of the required quality.

(*Financial Times*, 12/11/79)

The men were eventually sacked with very little protest from the union. At almost the same time in Cuba ...

The President's brother (General Raul Castro) was courageous enough to confess that Cuba's ills could not all be blamed on the US blockade, the crisis of capitalism, or the wrath of nature, however often they may have been 'used as pretexts to hide our deficiencies'.

To the objective factors we have described we must add the presence of indiscipline, irresponsibility, complacency, negligence, and 'buddyism' which, in addition to aggravating many problems, prevent others from being solved and generate justified irritation on the part of broad sectors of the population.

Particularly in agriculture, Sr Castro charged, many people were working only four to six hours a day. The norm system was being widely abused, with people fulfilling their norm two or three times over in one day and then knocking off for two days. There was unwillingness to overfill norms lest they be increased.

(*Financial Times*, 22/1/80)

We see these processes as something to be encouraged rather than suppressed. In such incidents we find the nucleus of the possibility of a social return. In the process of production, workers are well placed to enhance the effectiveness of machines and to spot obvious improvements in both the process and the product. Wilkinson (1983) gives a host of further examples of such direct forms of worker control. Quality Circles are a clear, and successful, attempt to parasitise this process in the search for profit.

To return to our example of JLD, why should we not ask, as a condition of our social investment in the technology, that JLD codifies its shop-floor and production line experience in winning free time. Workers usually find ways of wringing more out of a technology than the manufacturers imagine. They can often see directly how the technology could be enhanced. A codification of this experience and insight could be considered a deliverable, in a way that many of the social objectives are not. It has the properties of being able to cross the boundary of the organization, and of being able to act as an input to the meta-system. It is a social return that actually is returned.

The meta-system would thereby build up its bank of experience in dealing with individual enterprises, its social capital. It would also, by virtue of its size and position, be able to start bringing pressure to bear on the manufacturers of the means of production to modify the technology in a humanizing direction. Influencing and ultimately controlling the manufacture of the means of production is in our view necessary, without which a socialist state cannot hope to realise a transformation of the work process.

In practice, a historical approximation to this idea was GLEB's Technology Network strategy. This included the creation of a product-bank of innovations developed by the networks, although it is unclear whether this was to be built upon the experience of the enterprises and workers involved, or just on the networks themselves.

In our example, another form of social return could be the development of the technology itself. Patents, designs, innovations, 'know how', and 'good practice' return to the authority as a form of social accumulation. The developed technology is a 'deliverable' in the same way as the codification of experience. 'Know how' and 'good practice' are codifications of experience, in the sense we have already used it. All of this can then be used '(re-invested') in the restructuring of other enterprises.

Part of the authority's intervention in enterprises will be helping to define social and technological need. The accumulated social capital will contribute towards defining and meeting needs. In this case, the returns flowing back to the authority from previous social investments strengthen its ability to carry out future interventions.

Within JLD, it is easy to imagine this same agreement - a social return that codifies experience - having beneficial effects. It would in principle be very difficult to generate this return without the involvement of shop floor workers. Their experience is the basis of the return. Involving the shop floor in an area where *their competence* is at a premium would probably entail a generalized increase in self-confidence, and probably increase innovation and the democratization of control - two social objectives that are now approached indirectly through investment criteria and social return. Similar processes could be expected if the company were private, with an enterprise plan, rather than a cooperative.

The notion of agreed social return has another aspect. It can be produced as a development from an existing social momentum. Social objectives introduced from the outside can easily collide with the existing organizational momentum. We saw earlier in the stories from Leyland and Cuba that management tends to take a negative or at best ambivalent attitude towards worker creativity. Yet this is an attempt to beat organizational momentum that is usually dommed to failure. So a social return is built on organizational momentum, rather than colliding with it. As we said earlier, it also acts as an input to the strategic authority, building the bank of experience, and facilitating further broader social changes. In other words, the *social return has an impact outside the organization*.

In our example, JLD would agree to codify its experience in humanizing production, in winning free time, and in generally enhancing the technology. This codification would be the return that was expected from the social investment. The meta-system (Government, Strategic Authority) could then use this 'return' to improve its other interventions.

This is not just a question of increasing its experience. Comparison of social returns from different social investments would enable planners - including 'popular planners' - to identify future social investment areas. Thus social return acts rather like profit - defined as rate of return on capital. It allows future investment to be directed. It provides a mechanism for the allocation of social capital in the same way profit does for private capital[6]. We believe mechanisms of this sort happen in practice, in resource allocation and social investment decisions. However they happen in an *ad hoc* way. Confusions can and do arise when social objectives are seen as returns.

If the idea of 'return' is not made explicit, it may appear that investments are not getting anywhere - are 'unprofitable'. In fact, there may be a good social return when objectives are not met. Conversely, objectives may be met, but no return provided to the investing authority. Such a confusion of objectives and return can lead to calls for the restoration of profit and financial performance as the evaluative criteria as has more recently been the case at GLEB.

More importantly, at its own level, it could start to bring pressure to bear on the manufacturers of the means of production to change their product in a way that allowed more humanization of the work process; more shop floor control. Thus social factors would start to be included in the design of the means of production. The pressures on technology design for deskilling, task fragmentation, and control centralization would begin to balanced by other pressures.

Even partial redesign of the means of production in a small number of sectors would start an important process. Private enterprise would be subjected to social pressures inherent in the technology. The situation where cooperatives and other socially owned enterprises continually import the needs of capital in the Trojan Horse of technology might be slowed or even reversed.

Summary and conclusions

In this paper we have focused on the problems of technology and the possibilities of transofming the technology to illustrate the central idea of social return. It should not be difficult to construct further examples in the area of equal opportunities or socially useful products that follow similar lines. Probably the best example is the Lucas Plan. This could have been a purely internal development. As such it would still have met all sorts of good social objectives. The fact is that the codification of the Lucas Experience provided a vehicle that crossed the boundaries of the enterprise, and had a much wider social impact. The Lucas Plan was a sort of pre-figurative social return. The experience of the KME cooperative illustrates what can happen without defined social returns. When the cooperative was established, with inadequate financial assistance from the state, the shop stewards adopted the management role. In the process the cooperative failed to develop any democratic structure (Clarke, 1978; Eccles, 1981) and while there was a great deal of commitment from the workforce to the cooperative, their work experience remained largely unchanged. Again it is easy to speculate on the counterfactual. What processes could have emerged within KME if there had been a defined social return, in addition to social objectives?

We have pursued an analogy of social investment and social return. The social return is definable; subject to agreement; crosses the boundary of the organization; and acts as an input to the body making the social investment.

The notion of social return was often approached in practice by the Greater London Enterprise Board and the London Cooperative Enterprise Board. We hope it has been helpful to clarify the concept, and especially to distinguish it from social objectives.

In conclusion we observe that economic investment and the pursuit of economic return as usually practised often has negative social consequences inside and outside the enterprise; speedup and redundancy; control centralization and job fragmentation; stress and alienation. In opposition to this we believe that social constraints and returns should have positive organizational effects: organizational effectiveness and product quality; shop floor control and work process humanization; decreasing stress and greater satisfaction. In addition, a social return gives the investing authority the necessary bank of understanding to undertake further infrastructural interventions - to constantly extend the practice of restructuring for labour.

Footnotes

(1) Clearly technology does not <u>determine</u> relations of production. It does create very strong constraints on the types of organization and consciousness that is possible. The term that best describes the social forces brought to bear on a particular enterprise - the way it is 'kept in line' - is '<u>insistence</u>'.

(2) Social objectives may not necessarily clash with commercial criteria and market viability. Enterprises with non-profit maximizing objectives may find ways of surviving. The amrket itself is 'not an undifferentiated entity but a complex of relations which impose constraints of varying vigour and arbitrariness' (Clarke, 1984, 104). The wide range of experiences of cooperatives in different sectors is an example. But in general, social objectives oppose many of the imperatives of capitalist production - and in the short-term most involve extra time and money.

(3) If it is, there is no reason why loan funds cannot be made available at, or near commercial rates. Even a commercially viable venture may have problems obtaining conventional finance. Banks do not view all applicants equally. Those with sound projects, but who are not experienced in culturally acceptable self-presentation (cooperatives, ethnic minorities) may suffer discrimination. For them, loans from public authorities at commercial rates should be acceptable.

(4) Although we do not go into detail here, a more ambitious consideration of social return would be related to the allocation of resources. One of the functions of profit in a capitalist economy is the allocation of capital: capital flows from investments which yield low profit to

those which yield a higher profit. Underlying the
strategy of restructuring for labour is a rejection of
profit, both as the embodiment of surplus value and as a
means of allocating 'resources'. If profitability is not
to be the criteria for investment, an alternative must be
developed.

If investment is directed to social objectives,
then some form of social return criteria must be used to
direct investment towards one use rather than another.
This question has been aired elsewhere (Whitbread, 1984)
but remains relatively underdeveloped. It will need to
be addressed in the context of economic development for
social objectives.

(5) The GLC analysed the existing mechanisms of power in
large manufacturing and retail chains (GLC, 1985a, 36).
The power of coordination and fast response was often -
even inevitably - based on an infrastructure of computers
and electronic media. Information was the basis of
crurical higher level mechanisms of coordination and
control. This was a role that the GLC undertook itself.

(6) In this paper we have moved from social investments to
introduce social objectives and social returns. Although
we have developed some analogies between social and
financial investments, the two represent distinctly
different political economies. They have different ends
in view, as well as different process of reaching those
ends. Financial investments are a reflection of
valuations of objectivs in the market, which in turn are
a reflection of the prevailing structure of power in the
market. They represent the economics of capital. Social
investments are part of a process of restructuring for
labour, representing a different valuation of the
objectives of investment and a different political
economy.

The differences between social and financial investments are closely linked to the plan versus market debate. If it is accepted that the market is in general an efficient way of allocating resources, then the preferred way of allocating capital resources is through conventional financial investment criteria, in which profitability of an investment is the key. One of the functions of profit in a capitalist economy is the allocation of capital; capital flows from investments which yield low profit to those which yield a higher profit. For 'pro-marketeers', the only question to be addressed is how to make markets efficient, including the pricing of externalities.

Underlying the strategy of restructuring for labour is a rejection of the power of capital, including its transmission through the amrket. Integral to this is a rejection of profit, both as the embodiment of surplus value and as a means of allocating resoruces. The economics of labour attempts to counter the power of capital, but cannot rely on market processes to achieve this. The GLC and other metropolitan authorities recognized this and concentrated on regaining control through planning. In allocating resources towards the achievement of these objectives, then social returns become inputs to the planning process. Ultimately the question of criteria for social investment must be addressed. If profitability is not to be the criteria for investment, however, an alternative must be developed; if investment is to be directed towards social objectives, then some form of social return criteria must be used to allocate investment towards one use rather than another.

References

Braverman, H. (1974) *Labour and Monopoly Capitalism*, Monthly Review Press.

Clarke, T. (1978) *A Comparative Study of Three Major Workers Cooperatives*, SSRC Final Report.

Clarke, T. (1984) 'Alternative Modes of Cooperative Production', in *Economic and Industrial Democracy*, vol 5, pp 97-129.

Coates, K. (1981) *Work-ins, Sit-ins and Industrial Democracy*, Spokesman Books.

Eaton, J. (1979) 'The Basque Workers Cooperatives', *Industrial Relations Journal*, vol 10, no 3, pp 32-48.

Eccles, A. (1981) *Under New Management*, Pan.

Fine, B. and Harris, L. (1985) *The Peculiarities of the British Economy*, Lawrence and Wishart.

Greater London Council (1983) *Jobs For A Change*, GLC.

Greater London Council (1985a) *The London Industrial Strategy*, GLC.

Greater London Council (1985b) *GLC Social and Economic Study Pack no 5*, section II, paper 3, GLC.

Greater London Enterprise Board (1984) *A Strategy for Cooperation - Worker Cooperatives in London*, GLEB.

Gordon, D. (1976) 'Capitalist Efficiency and Socialist Efficiency', *Monthly Review*, July (1976).

Marx, K. (1976) *The First International and After*, Penguin.

Murray, R. (1985) 'Benetton Britain - The New Economic Order', *Marxism Today*, November (1985).

Rosenbrock, H. (1983) 'Designing Automated Systems - Need Skill be Lost?', *Science and Public Policy*, vol 10, no 16, pp 274-7.

Rowthorn, B. and Ward, T. (1983) 'How to Run a Business and Run Down an Economy: The Effects of Closing Down Steel-making in Corby', *Cambridge Journal of Economics*, vol 3, no 4.

Whitbread, D. (1985) 'Gorz, Nove and Hodgson: The Economics of Socialism', *Capital and Class* 26, CSE.

Wilkinson, B. (1983) *The Shopfloor Politics of New Technology*, Gower.